T0288279

CONCISE
LINCOLN
LIBRARY

—

EDITED BY RICHARD W. ETULAIN
AND SYLVIA FRANK RODRIGUE

RON J. KELLER

Lincoln in the Illinois Legislature

Southern Illinois University Press
Carbondale

Southern Illinois University Press
www.siupress.com

22 21 20 19   4 3 2 1

The Concise Lincoln Library has been made possible
in part through a generous donation by the Leland E.
and LaRita R. Boren Trust.
    Volumes in this series have been published with sup-
port from the Abraham Lincoln Bicentennial Foundation, dedicated to perpetuating and expanding Lincoln's vision for America and completing America's
unfinished work.

Jacket illustration adapted from a painting by Wendy
Allen

Library of Congress Cataloging-in-Publication Data
Names: Keller, Ron J., 1969– author.
Title: Lincoln in the Illinois legislature / Ron J. Keller.
Description: Carbondale : Southern Illinois Univer-
sity Press, [2019] | Series: Concise Lincoln library |
Includes bibliographical references and index.
Identifiers: LCCN 2018024034 | ISBN 9780809337002
(cloth : alk. paper) | ISBN 9780809337019 (e-book)Sub-
jects: LCSH: Lincoln, Abraham, 1809–1865—Political
career before 1861. | Illinois. General Assembly. House
of Representatives. | Legislators—Illinois—Biography. |
Illinois—Politics and government—To 1865.
Classification: LCC E457.35 .K45 2019 |
DDC 328.773092 [B] —dc23 LC record available at
https://lccn.log.gov/2018024034

Printed on recycled paper. ♻
This paper meets the requirements of ANSI/NISO
Z39.48-1992 (Permanence of Paper) ∞

To my wife, Cindy,
and my children, Josiah, Ethan, and Annagrace,
for all their love and support

And to my high school history teacher Dave Thompson,
who inculcated in me a love and appreciation for the world of history

CONTENTS

ILLUSTRATIONS

PREFACE

In 1841 near the end of his time in the Illinois legislature, Abraham Lincoln confided to his friend Joshua Speed that he had longed to achieve something of lasting significance. Lincoln had served as state legislator for seven years by that time and may have hoped that his legislative achievements would have afforded him a legacy. But history has not extended him that privilege. Lincoln's four terms in the Illinois House of Representatives are largely brushed over by biographers, and historians have mostly regarded Lincoln's years in the statehouse as less important than his budding law career and circuit-riding days or the drama of his relationships with Ann Rutledge, Mary Owens, and Mary Todd. Lincoln's single and largely ineffective term as U.S. congressman from 1847 to 1849 often garners more attention than his four transformative terms as Illinois state representative from 1834 to 1842.

Lincoln himself is partly to blame for this oversight. In the autobiographies he wrote for Charles Lanman and Jesse Fell in 1858 and 1859, he devoted only four total sentences to his legislative service. One sentence relays his defeat the first time he ran for office. Another matter-of-factly states that he was not a candidate after four terms. He gives not one mention in those two autobiographies to any piece of legislation in which he participated in his eight years as state representative. Only in his 1860 autobiography for John L. Scripps does Lincoln mention a single legislative act: his 1837 protest on the slavery question.

In part, historians have omitted Lincoln's legislative years because his record was less than stellar. Aside from legislation brought forth by

committees of which he was a member, of the 1,647 bills that passed
during those years, Lincoln introduced only thirty total bills, resolutions, and petitions.[1] And the one issue he most ardently championed
and shepherded through the legislature—the internal improvements
system—left the state drowning in debt for more than a generation.

Yet Lincoln's time in the Illinois General Assembly was instrumental. The people he met laid his political foundation. He developed,
honed, and displayed in those years the qualities and characteristics
that have become so closely associated with him: honesty, empathy,
leadership, and political vision. And the years of Lincoln's tenure in
the state legislature were critical for the development of the state of
Illinois.

Lincoln's legislative experiences have been the focus of a major
book only once: the highly acclaimed *Lincoln's Preparation for Greatness: The Illinois Legislative Years* (1965) by the late former Illinois
state representative and U.S. senator Paul Simon. (Although Richard
Lawrence Miller's 2008 *Prairie Politician* almost qualifies, it was
part of a four-volume work). Fifty years later, it is time to reconsider
Lincoln's legislative years. It is my honor to write a follow-up to Simon, in which, on a few occasions, I break with his conclusions. My
assessment of Lincoln as the logrolling legislator in 1837, for instance,
is less sympathetic. And more than Simon did, I have stressed Lincoln's economic vision as a driver of his policies and his philosophy
and have set national politics within the landscape of state politics.
I have highlighted the personal character of Lincoln as well as the
relationships he forged in his years as a legislator. I hope this book
will be useful as an examination of Lincoln's early political career
and the art of early Illinois legislative politics. Equally, I hope the
book contributes to our understanding of this formative period in
the life of one of our greatest Americans.

I wish to express my sincere gratitude to all the generous institu-
tions and individuals who assisted in my research. I thank Richard
Sumrall and staff at Lincoln Public Library; Daniel Weinberg at the
Abraham Lincoln Book Shop; Anne Moseley at the Lincoln Heritage
Museum; James Cornelius, Kathryn Harris, Roberta Fairburn, and

Jenny Ericson at the Abraham Lincoln Presidential Library and Museum; Wayne Temple at the Illinois State Archives; Daniel Stowell and Daniel Worthington at the Papers of Abraham Lincoln; Sara Gabbard and Adriana Maynard of the Allen County (Indiana) Public Library; Dale Ogden of the Indiana State Museum; Justin Blanford and staff at the Old State Capitol Historic Site; Cathy Smith at the Evans Public Library in Vandalia; Steve Riddle and Linda Hanabarger at the Vandalia State House Historic Site; Steve Durbin at the Fayette County Museum; and Walter Ray, archivist with the Special Collections Research Center at Southern Illinois University. Thanks to Mike Meador, Ronald C. White Jr., Robert Shaw, Guy Fraker, Frank Williams, and Harold Holzer for their scholarly suggestions and encouragement. I thank Sylvia Frank Rodrigue with Southern Illinois University Press for her invaluable assistance throughout this project and Richard Etulain, Concise Lincoln Library series co-editor, Judy Verdich, Linda Buhman, Wayne Larsen, and Lisa Marty at SIU Press for their counsel. Thank you to the anonymous reviewers who provided feedback in making this a stronger work. I thank Lincoln College for granting a sabbatical leave for me to conduct my research and writing. I thank the Lord for His continual abundant blessings. Thank you to my wonderful family, my wife, Cindy, and children Josiah, Ethan, and Annagrace for their love and support.

LINCOLN IN THE ILLINOIS LEGISLATURE

Earliest known photograph of Abraham Lincoln. This image of Lincoln was taken in Springfield, probably in 1846 after he was elected to Congress. Courtesy of Library of Congress.

CITIZEN LINCOLN,
CANDIDATE LINCOLN

O n a sweltering summer day in 1831 a tall, twenty-two-year-old
man sauntered into the small log-cabin settlement of New
Salem, Illinois. He knew only local entrepreneur Denton Offutt,
who had hired him a few months prior to help pilot a flatboat of
goods down the Mississippi River to New Orleans. Abraham Lincoln
entered the village with high hopes, looking for the opportunity to
establish himself there and rise in achievement. He had chosen a life
different from his father, whose narrow ambition, limited education,
and traditional worldview were at odds with young Lincoln's aims.
So he left his father's homestead on the prairie in Coles County, Illinois, and traveled over a hundred miles northwest to New Salem—a
village of approximately a hundred residents near the center of the
state. It was a modest beginning to Lincoln's life of independence.
Yet within a year he would launch his political career for the state
legislature, and in less than ten years would be known statewide.

Denton Offutt had met Lincoln in early February and in March
had hired him and his stepbrother John Johnston to help construct
a flatboat to take supplies down to New Orleans. They loaded the
flatboat and maneuvered it down the Sangamon River. But in the
shallow waters at New Salem, the boat protruded over a dam and
became stuck. Curious to see the activity, a crowd gathered as Lincoln
drilled a hole in the boat's bow to release the water that had seeped
in. His ingenuity pleased the onlookers, who applauded Lincoln's

resourcefulness. Offutt, who was also impressed, told Lincoln that he intended to open a store in New Salem, and asked if the young man might consider moving to the village to be his store clerk.

Taking Offutt up on his offer, Lincoln arrived in New Salem a "friendless, uneducated, penniless boy," as he later described himself.[1] He toted all that he owned under his arm. Upon gazing at the tall, lanky newcomer, New Salem resident William Butler pronounced him "as ruff a specimen of humanity as could be found. His legs were bare for six inches between bottom of pants and top of socks."[2] At six feet, four inches, dark-complexioned, with coarse, unruly black hair, he weighed only some 180 pounds, despite his great height.[3] His odd appearance was deceiving, for beneath the raggedness lay ambition, talent, and an intellect that would soon become apparent. But surely no one gazing upon this man in 1831 might predict the pinnacle of greatness and the place in history he would achieve. Indeed, in less than a decade after his arrival in New Salem, Abraham Lincoln would develop and display the admirable characteristics and qualities that defined him for the rest of his life.

Even in his extreme homeliness, Lincoln did not entirely stand out from the dwellers of his new hometown. Most of the inhabitants of New Salem were farmers originally from the South, many hailing, as Lincoln did, from Kentucky. Although small, the town boasted all the needed craftsmen and laborers necessary to frontier life, including a blacksmith, cabinetmaker, cobbler, cooper, hatter, two physicians, and a wheelwright. The town also had a court, post office, ferry, tavern, two stores, and two saloons. Independent and self-reliant, the villagers were typical of those described by a traveler to Illinois who noted that "they have much plain, blunt, but sincere hospitality . . . [and] assume no airs of distinction."[4] As was typical of a raw pioneer village, a large number of roughs and bullies inhabited New Salem.[5]

Physical strength proved valuable on the frontier. Not long after arriving, Lincoln encountered a test of his manhood against the town ruffians—the Clary's Grove Boys. The group's leader, Jack Armstrong, challenged him to a wrestling match. It is unclear who prevailed in the bout. Both men fought hard, and Lincoln's strength and confidence were enough to win the good will and respect of Armstrong and his followers. The match yielded for Lincoln more than admiration for his physical prowess: these very men befriended and later defended Lincoln, aiding him in his political rise.

Despite its hard side, New Salem possessed educated citizens, and Lincoln found favor among that company as well. At least six college graduates lived in New Salem, along with a few free thinkers, toward whom Lincoln gravitated. Wishing to compensate for his own deficiencies after having had just a year of formal education in Kentucky and Indiana, he sought out the local schoolmaster Mentor Graham, the town philosopher Jack Kelso, and the justice of the peace Bowling Green. Lincoln borrowed books from the town mill owner and tavern keeper, James Rutledge, who had a personal library. He picked the brain of Dartmouth graduate Dr. John Allen on religious topics. It was in New Salem that Lincoln encountered the literature of Shakespeare, the poetry of Robert Burns, and the Enlightenment philosophy of Thomas Paine.

Of all his fellow citizens, Green had the greatest long-term impact on Lincoln politically; the eager student became fascinated with elements of law after Green gave Lincoln the opportunity to participate in court proceedings, arguing small court cases without pay.[6] Green had previously served as a canal commissioner and knew the ins and outs of canal building, and this knowledge would also prove useful to Lincoln.[7]

Lincoln's physical strength, budding intellect, genial demeanor, and boisterous sense of humor won him many friends in New Salem. For the goodwill and amusement of others he was always ready with a joke or tall tale. But acquaintances quickly recognized, as villager Jason Duncan did, that beyond a penchant to amuse, Lincoln possessed intelligence "far beyond . . . his age."[8]

The intellectually curious Lincoln began regularly to attend meetings of the New Salem Debating Society. From his first appearance at a society meeting, he impressed the participants with his natural ability to communicate and enthrall. James Rutledge, president of the society, recalled that as Lincoln stood for open discussion, he thrust his hands deep into the pockets of his pantaloons. Attendees smiled with anticipation, expecting a yarn from the awkwardly posed speaker, who astonished them with an intellectual treatise. Observing Lincoln lost in debate, surrounded by an enraptured audience, Rutledge concluded that "there was more in Abe's head than wit and fun; that he was already a fine speaker; that all he lacked was culture to enable him to reach the high destiny which he knew was in store for him."[9]

Indeed, Lincoln had a keen interest in politics. In 1830 after his father relocated from Indiana to Macon County, Illinois, Lincoln witnessed political stump speaking for the first time. He stood mesmerized by the sight of William Lee Ewing and John F. Posey, canvassing for the state legislature, using the power of words and ideas to charm a crowd.[10] The speeches impressed him so much that he afterward took to the stump to make his own speech, much to the amusement of the assembly.[11]

Now on August 1, 1831, just weeks after his arrival in New Salem, voters cast their ballots for U.S. Congress. In the home of James Camron, Lincoln likely cast a vote for the first time in his life. In keeping with the common practice of elections at that time, he voted orally, announcing his choices to the clerks of election who sat behind a table marking their tally sheets.[12] In Illinois, all white male inhabitants who had achieved twenty-one years of age and resided in the state six months preceding the election were eligible to vote.[13] The convergence of elective politics, community relationships, and civic spirit presented an opportunity for an ambitious political enthusiast like Lincoln. Making the most of the experience, he dawdled at the polling place long after he voted, greeting neighbors, and, by nightfall, the relative newcomer had met nearly all the men from the surrounding area.[14]

Lincoln deepened his involvement in community affairs by offering to help his neighbors raise houses or harvest crops. His propensity for honesty and reputation for impartiality prompted villagers to solicit his assistance in judging footraces and other local contests. Townsfolk called upon this man of character when they needed someone of intellect, such as when Lincoln was asked to petition the county court to help a local man who had gone insane.[15] Within months, it was said Lincoln "knew every man, woman & child for miles around."[16]

In the year following his arrival in New Salem, Lincoln continued to clerk in Offutt's store, earning a decent salary of fifteen dollars a month and lodging in the back room. While Lincoln was grateful for the job, the twenty-three-year-old aspired to something greater. "He talked about politics Considerable," observed one New Salem resident.[17] With his talents and ambition, Lincoln believed politics could be a ticket to making a name for himself and rising in the world. A seat in the Illinois state legislature held great appeal. Members enjoyed prominence in their respective communities, and the office was attainable by anyone willing to campaign hard enough. By early 1832 Lincoln had lived in the region for less than nine months, but felt his prospects might be favorable. He floated the idea of a legislative candidacy to a few of his fellow residents, including James Rutledge, who advised Lincoln that a run for elective office might bring him "before the people and in time would do him good."[18]

Others thought the idea of uncouth, ill-dressed, and inexperienced Lincoln as state representative a joke, and did not expect his candidacy to materialize.[19] But most residents, "with warm solicitations," hailed the thought.[20] New Salem resident J. Rowan Herndon voiced the sentiments of many in the village declaring that the people "had a wright to a member [of the legislature] from that Part of the County."[21] "Encouraged," as he put it, "by his great popularity among his immediate neighbors," Lincoln forwarded his name as a candidate for the state legislature on March 9, 1832, in a circular appearing in the Springfield newspaper, the *Sangamo Journal*.[22]

Announcing one's candidacy in the newspaper was a common practice for novice candidates. With no real national party organization established by 1832, a man seeking political office might be fortunate enough to enjoy the backing of influential politicians or have a large group of supporters create an announcement on his behalf. As a newcomer, Lincoln had no influential backers. So in accordance with the expectation of first-time applicants, he composed a statement of his principles and beliefs, and outlined how he might serve the constituents of the district. He may have printed and distributed handbills, but none survives. Realizing the imperfections of his writing, Lincoln called upon others, particularly Mentor Graham—who had instructed his student already on the finer points of grammar—for assistance in writing his announcement.[23]

Introducing himself to many residents would be crucial. Because of its sheer size and population, Sangamon County constituted the largest share of members of the legislature of any county in the state. In 1832 the county included the present-day counties of Logan and Menard as well as part of Mason and most of Christian. The size of the constituency entitled Sangamon to four representatives. Lincoln would be competing against twelve other candidates, and he realized the uphill battle he would face. "I am young and unknown to many of you," he frankly admitted to audiences.[24] Knowing the odds against him, Lincoln did not hold high hopes for a victory. In fact, essentially conceding defeat long before voting began, Lincoln stated unpretentiously that "if the good people in their wisdom shall see fit to keep me in the background, I have been too familiar with disappointments to be very much chagrined."[25]

Lincoln's station in life gave him no reason to brag. His announcement struck a tone characteristically associated with Lincoln: "I was born and have ever remained in the most humble walks of life," he wrote, adding, "I have no wealthy or popular relations to recommend me."[26] Lincoln depicted himself as a man of poor and lowly means, a shrewd and deliberate maneuver to resonate with the frontier folk who resented elitist politicians. Throughout his political career, Lincoln would allude to his humble origins when convenient.

Regarding his platform, Lincoln quipped, "My politicks are short and sweet, like the old Womans dance."[27] He focused on a few issues of most concern to the citizens of the county: educational opportunity, a nod to the more learned voters in the region; internal improvements, such as improved transportation facilities; and a law against excessive interest rates.

"Upon the subject of education," the candidate wrote, "I can only say that I view it as the most important subject which we as a people can be engaged in."[28] Even though he offered no formal plan, Lincoln pointed out that education should be sufficient enough that any person "may duly appreciate the value of our free institutions," and may be learned enough to be "able [to] read the scriptures and other works, both of a religious and moral nature."[29] A strong advocacy for education should not be surprising from a voracious reader such as Lincoln. However, the frontier did not generally value education, as shown by the low literacy rate. At the very least, Lincoln hoped that through exposure to reading and education, people might learn and appreciate the significance of what the founding patriots had fought and bled for just a few generations ago. He longed to see the nation embrace education, and argued for a direct connection between education and "morality, sobriety, enterprise and industry."[30] His statements on works of religion and morality were acknowledgments that the Bible served as a requisite moral guide and was the most important literary staple in the Illinois frontier cabin, just as it had been for him as a youth in Kentucky and Indiana.

Lincoln devoted the bulk of his announcement to the benefits of internal improvements—particularly the dredging of the Sangamon River to make it navigable for steamboat travel. He hoped that cutting through some of the bends of the river would result in a deeper waterway that would not clog with driftwood, preventing boats from getting stuck, as he had the year before on his way to New Orleans. Lincoln saw that New Salem's survival depended upon the navigation of the Sangamon River. Simply put, poor, rural farmers needed a convenient and inexpensive way to get their products to distant markets. Cheaper and improved river transportation might be the only way for the subsistence farmers and small merchants of central Illinois to participate in wider commerce, enlarging their contact with other parts of the country and helping to lift them out of poverty. Greater commerce equaled greater progress. Lincoln positioned himself as an expert, writing in the newspaper announcement, "I have given as particular attention to the stage of the water in this river, as any other person in the country."[31] Understanding that the nation had begun to turn toward the new railroads, he contended that the "heart-appalling" expense of building railroads hindered their practicality. He vowed, "I believe the improvement of the Sangamon River to be vastly important and highly desirable to the people of this county; and if elected, any measure in the legislature having this for its object, which may appear judicious, will meet my approbation, and shall receive my support."[32]

Lincoln was not alone in pinning his hopes on the navigability of the Sangamon. The recent exciting arrival of a steamer up the river still resonated in people's minds. In January 1832 the area had received an announcement that Captain Vincent Bogue of Springfield intended to charter a small steamer named the *Talisman*, pilot it up the Illinois River to Beardstown, Illinois, then sail up the Sangamon River as soon as it thawed. A successful navigation of the Sangamon would demonstrate the feasibility of its commercial travel. When in mid-March Bogue arrived at Beardstown, he enlisted the support of men from New Salem and Springfield to ready the steamboat's safe passage by breaking the winter ice and clearing obstructions along the riverbed. Lincoln and several others volunteered and spent several chilly days breaking through ice at the Sangamon entrance, cutting off overhanging limbs and clearing snags in the stream. Just north of Springfield, a crowd cheered the approaching *Talisman*, many seeing a steamboat for the first time. At the trip's completion, experienced boatman Rowan Herndon hired Lincoln as an assistant to steer the steamer back to Beardstown, and, at New Salem, to help dismantle part of the dam to allow the boat to pass. Though Bogue's venture failed financially, to the public the mission demonstrated success: the prospect of reliable transportation might be fulfilled.[33] Lincoln's involvement in the *Talisman* venture gave his friends even more cause to encourage his legislative aspirations.[34]

In addition to championing education and internal improvements, Lincoln opposed high usury rates, or the common practice of loaning money at exorbitant interest. Settlers on the frontier, most of whom did not possess ready capital, had to rely on credit if they wished to enjoy economic opportunities and improve themselves. But they were often charged high interest rates on those loans, a system that Lincoln decried as "baneful and corroding" because it prevented the poor farmer from ever rising out of his economic station.[35] Lincoln knew about borrowing on interest. When Offutt opened his shop in 1831, the storekeeper had to borrow $110 dollars at a whopping

60 percent interest.[36] Advocating the cause of the common man, Lincoln suggested that a law prohibiting usurious interest rates "may be made, without materially injuring any class of people." It would be an avenue to allow the poor to rise without fear of exploitation, a core economic tenet for Lincoln. Several years later, in a speech before the legislature, he would decry the tactics of the wealthy capitalists, whom he condemned for their desire to "generally act harmoniously, and in concert, to fleece the people."[37]

Lincoln's early political outlook rested principally on an economic vision: through hard work, self-discipline, education, and social respectability, one could attain a higher place in society and improve his station in life. Lincoln also aligned himself with the notion that government support of new technology and inventions would bring progress for all. Lincoln maintained that assertive and progressive state and federal government action could help the general welfare of all people. He would later write that "the legitimate object of government is to do for the people whatever needs to be done, but which they cannot, by individual effort, do at all or do so well, for themselves."[38] Lincoln believed that active governmental support— specifically of internal improvements and education—was the best vehicle to lift economic burdens from the shoulders of the citizens of the Illinois frontier.

This first outline of Lincoln's stances was, to him, much more than a campaign statement. In it he articulated a vision and outlined his political dogma, proposing ideas that would remain central to his economic philosophy and guide him throughout his political career. Education could be the key to social and personal upward mobility. Government support of internal improvements and other enterprises could transform the state and the country into a successful, commercially oriented society. Low-interest rates could make capital available for improvements of all sorts. Through those government-endorsed efforts, a greater economic opportunity could be extended to a larger number of people—strengthening their standing, their lives, and the whole country's welfare. These principles were, to Lincoln, his generation's mandate for shaping the country's future.[39]

Lincoln concluded his campaign address with a personal desire: "Every man is said to have his peculiar ambition. Whether it be true or not, I can say for one that I have no other so great as that of being truly esteemed of my fellow men, by rendering myself worthy of their esteem."[40] Perhaps no other statement in that announcement—or any statement he would make in his entire life—might best illustrate his measure of success. A man could stand out by proving himself and should receive respect only through deserving and earning it. As he would later demonstrate, Lincoln held that winning of esteem should not be for one's own advancement alone, but rather in order to forward causes that would advance mankind.

Although the political party system had not yet become fully entrenched, by 1832 partisanship was common. Men identified with and aligned themselves behind well-known political leaders of the era, particularly President Andrew Jackson, who was running for a second term, and Jackson's nemesis in Congress, Senator Henry Clay. Frontier voters based their allegiances on the regional popularity of a given politician or upon the specific issues the leader espoused. In Illinois, Jackson claimed the mantle of hero of the frontier. The majority of Illinoisans in 1832 divided themselves politically into one of two camps: they were either for Jackson or against Jackson, though even among Jackson supporters, some were more fervent about his policies than others. The valiant victor of the Battle of New Orleans had made a name for himself as the champion of the common man, rejecting the elitist notions of previous Virginia and Massachusetts presidents. He portrayed himself as the protector of agrarians, fighting against business interests that he depicted as immoral and self-serving. Jackson's Indian Removal Act of 1830, his stand against Southern firebrands over the right to nullify tariff laws, and his public battles with Congress—especially over the rechartering of the Bank of the United States—endeared him to those in central Illinois. The Jackson faithful organized themselves behind their man, and, by 1832, they began referring to themselves as the Democratic Party. Their success lay in their support for extending the right of suffrage to all adult white male citizens, not just those who owned property. This support brought many common people from the frontier into their tent.[41]

President Jackson often found himself at odds with Congress, chiefly Kentucky senator Henry Clay. As early as 1816, Clay had made a name for himself in the U.S. Senate, trumpeting the "American System." This activist economic program called for federal government funding for large-scale internal improvements in infrastructure, primarily roads, bridges, and canals. When Jackson ran for president in 1824, in a race thrown to the U.S. House of Representatives to decide, Clay as Speaker of the House backed John Quincy Adams, helping to defeat Jackson. Jackson showed no forgiveness, and after he captured the presidency four years later, he targeted Clay and attempted to derail the senator's beloved internal improvements plan. In turn, Clay criticized Jackson's expansion of presidential powers. He and other like-minded congressmen began referring to the president as "King Andrew." These opponents of Jackson and his Democrats coalesced into their own loose political party. Clay entered the presidential contest in 1832 against Jackson as a candidate for the upstart National Republican Party.[42]

While Jackson stood as the preferred candidate in Illinois, Clay also enjoyed a spate of followers. Lincoln counted himself among the Clay men. He approved of the senator's American System, and, like Clay, believed that government support for internal improvements—through both public and private expenditures—could serve as the vehicle to move the country toward economic progress. Lincoln also embraced the doctrines of the National Republicans (soon to be known as the Whigs) of a protective tariff, a national bank, and paper currency. Lincoln's admiration for Clay ran deep, and he referred to the senator as "my beau ideal of a statesman."[43] Although it is not certain if Clay and Lincoln ever met, the Kentucky senator's economic dogma would influence Lincoln's political ideas more than that of any other person.

Lincoln's campaign announcement echoed some of Clay's calls for internal improvements, but Lincoln largely stayed clear of thorny partisan issues. He knew it might be politically unwise to agitate a Jackson audience during a presidential election year. And, for a position as state representative, local issues were still paramount.[44]

Circuit-riding Methodist preacher Peter Cartwright presented himself as one of Lincoln's primary opponents. The Virginia-born

Cartwright had lived in Kentucky, where he became an ordained minister, before his religious objections to slavery prompted him to move to Illinois in 1824. Cartwright called himself "God's plowman" and made no apologies for his passionate religious revivals or his fervent attempts to convert the prairies to the gospel. He rode many miles on the circuit in central Illinois, encountering thousands of residents and establishing himself as one of the premier circuit-riding preachers in the Midwest. Cartwright and Lincoln first met in 1830 during Cartwright's unsuccessful gubernatorial candidacy. Now he squared off as a Democrat against Lincoln and other candidates for the state legislature.[45]

Lincoln wanted to debate the evangelist. He harbored skepticism of preachers and resented their propensity to play on people's emotions instead of their reason. After the shabbily dressed Lincoln and the dapper Cartwright met in 1832, they jumped into an impromptu discussion.[46] William Butler observed the encounter, and recalled that his "first special attention was attracted to Lincoln by the way in which he met the great preacher in his arguments, and the extensive acquaintance he showed with the politics of the State." Butler concluded that the outsider Lincoln "quite beat" Cartwright.[47]

Just a month after Lincoln made his candidacy official, he abruptly suspended his campaigning. In April 1832 news reached New Salem that a band of Fox and Sauk Indians under the leadership of Black Hawk had crossed over the Mississippi River from Iowa into Illinois. Black Hawk's tribes hoped to reclaim and reoccupy lands in northwestern Illinois that they had lost by a treaty some years before. The United States government considered Black Hawk's intentions hostile and called for volunteers in Illinois to leave their homes and fight the invading Indian forces. Lincoln felt the impulse to sign up. Besides, the Offutt store verged on failing, and he had no other employment. Although he had just announced his intention to seek a seat in the legislature, a sense of adventure prompted him to enroll in the Illinois Volunteers. He joined a number of the Clary's Grove boys, who elected him as the captain of the company. During his three-month stint, Lincoln saw no fighting but gained something of a view of a soldier's life and exercised practical leadership in his role as captain in a rifle company of the 31st Regiment. He met and befriended many, including John T. Stuart from Springfield. Lincoln would later poke fun at this war adventure, but it did earn him $124, which he needed at the time. More importantly, he concluded that leadership experience gave him "so much satisfaction."[48] Arriving back at New Salem at the end of July, Lincoln had just ten days to canvass the county as part of his campaign. Starting with a speech in Petersburg, he began traveling from village to village, addressing crowds where he could find them—at meetinghouses, public sales, or shooting matches. He would be fortunate to find captive audiences of twenty or so. He repeated his campaign themes of support for education, a national bank, and a protective tariff.[49] Above all, he pointed out to voters the great resources the state had and the "wonderful opportunities" that lay before them with internal improvements.[50] When the audience would drift off, he resorted to his ready wit and colloquial arguments to draw them back in.

Lincoln retained both his humble nature and appearance, not attempting to dress himself any differently from when he arrived in New Salem the year before. He wore a simple straw hat, no vest, a coat too small for his long arms, threadbare pants that ended five inches above his ankles, and often just one suspender holding up his pants.[51] Lincoln jokingly reveled in his homely look, and according to J. Rowan Herndon, he told an audience, "I have Been told that some of my opponents have said that it was a disgrase to the County of sangamon to have such a Looking man as i am stuck up for the Legislator now i thought this was a free Cuntry that is the Reason that i adress you to Day had i have Known to the Contrary i should Knot have Consented to Run."[52]

For the most part the political aspirant received a respectful welcome wherever he wandered. John Stuart recollected that Lincoln acquired through his canvassing "a reputation for candor and honesty" and that "he made friends everywhere he went."[53] William Butler recalled that people became easily attracted to Lincoln as a candidate simply because he was "a good fellow . . . genial, kind, sympathetic, and open-hearted."[54] Beyond his appearance, these new acquaintances discovered there was something more in him. New

Salem resident T. G. Onstot recalled that "Mr. Lincoln was dressed in a suit of jeans with heavy boots and looked like a farmer, and the people were very much surprised when they heard his speech."[55] In eastern Sangamon County, after hearing a local politician talk about navigation on the Sangamon River, Lincoln decided he knew as much as the politician. So Lincoln took a keg lying on its side, turned it up on end, leaped on top of it, and in the words of Lincoln's cousin John Hanks, "Abe beat him to death" in his speech.[56]

However, some places in the county remained rather hard territory, and candidates had to expect almost anything to transpire. At a stop at a sale in Pappsville, just as Lincoln took to the stump to speak, he noticed his friend Herndon being heckled. When the scene escalated into a fight, Lincoln stepped in to stop it. Pushing his way through the crowd, he grabbed the primary assailant by the neck and trousers and tossed him to the ground. The fight immediately ceased, and Lincoln, satisfied, jumped back onto the stump and commenced his speech right where he had left off: "Fellow citizens, I am humble Abraham Lincoln."[57]

Stephen T. Logan, a Springfield lawyer, recalled that of the contestants for the legislature that year, only Stuart and newcomer Lincoln attracted his attention. Logan described Lincoln as he saw him for the first time at a political rally at the courthouse in Springfield: "I saw Lincoln before he went up into the stand to make his speech. He was a very tall and gawky and rough looking fellow then . . . But after he began speaking I became very much interested in him. He made a very sensible speech . . . Up to that time I think he had been doing odd jobs of surveying, and one thing and another. But one thing we very soon learned was that he was immensely popular."[58]

Perhaps Lincoln garnered popularity, but with only four seats available, thirteen candidates running, and a short time to introduce himself to the county outside New Salem, he was unable to reach enough voters to win the election. He resigned himself to his fate. A supporter wrote of Lincoln's chances: "So little was Known of Mr. Lincoln by the inhabitants of Sangamon at the time he first became a candidate for the legislature that when a few miles out of town in my rides [I] would be asked who Abraham was."[59]

On August 6, 1832, voters cast their ballots for state representative and state senator. As expected, Lincoln did not win a seat, finishing eighth with 657 votes. The four candidates elected were Edmund D. Taylor, John T. Stuart, Achilles Morris, and Peter Cartwright.[60] But Lincoln relished his standing even in defeat. He garnered 277 out of 290 votes cast in New Salem—a more than respectable showing for a political upstart. The results were a testament to his geniality and character, and were tangible evidence of how hard he had worked to overcome his deficiencies in wealth, education, and connections. It would be the only time, he later proudly noted, that he would be beaten on a direct vote of the people.[61] In Lincoln's own estimation, even with the loss, this first campaign had done him "much good."[62] The experience had emboldened him, and won him valuable acquaintances, greater oratorical skill, and a zest for politics that would carry him forward for many years to come.

Note written by Lincoln. The first-term state legislator wrote to the Illinois House Speaker on December 1, 1834, about his intention to propose his first legislative bill. Courtesy of Illinois State Archives.

A PROMINENT AND
PARTISAN POLITICIAN

After his electoral loss in August 1832, Lincoln found himself again without income. Inclined to study law, he felt he did not know enough to succeed in that field. So in January 1833 Lincoln entered into a partnership with William Berry to open a store in New Salem. Lacking capital, they purchased store products on credit. Unfortunately neither man possessed business acumen, and they saw themselves, in Lincoln's words, "get deeper and deeper in debt."[1] Berry's death in 1835 left Lincoln saddled with the store's remaining debts, which totaled more than a thousand dollars, a large burden for his limited resources. It would take him nearly a decade to pay off what he called his "national debt."[2] By 1836 Lincoln purchased two lots in Springfield, however, so it seems that he may have recovered more quickly than previously thought.

Good fortune had come his way, however, in May 1833, when President Andrew Jackson made Lincoln village postmaster. Although "an avowed Clay man," Lincoln considered the Jackson appointment "too insignificant" to allow political differences to stand in the way of accepting the position.[3] He now earned a regular salary for the first time in his life. But the position brought more than income for the politically minded Lincoln. Through this job he became better acquainted with the residents of the area and had access to the newspapers that came through the post office. He read about national politics and public opinion with great interest. Since a postmaster salary paid too little to support him, later in the year Lincoln accepted a second job as assistant Sangamon County surveyor for John Calhoun that provided yet another means of connecting with residents. Lincoln and his new boss were familiar with each other, as they had served together in the Black Hawk War. While Calhoun declared himself one of the most prominent Jacksonians in the county, he assured Lincoln that no political commitment or favor would be expected in return for the job. Not only did their political dissimilarities not hinder their relationship, but Lincoln was delighted that Calhoun helped sharpen his thinking.[4]

The notion of another run for the Illinois House never left Lincoln. His strong support in New Salem established his right to run again in 1834, and his respectable first showing boosted his confidence. He was older, wiser, and more politically astute. Since he had run before, a new declaration of principles would not be necessary. His appearance and demeanor had changed little in two years. Meeting Lincoln on the campaign circuit in 1834, Sangamon County politician Robert L. Wilson observed that Lincoln "had nothing in his appearance that was marked or Striking, but when enlivened in conversation or engaged in telling . . . his countenance would brighten."[5] But Lincoln had used the time between campaigns to advance his oratorical abilities. His voice, detected one observer, contained a "clear, Shrill monotone Style of Speaking, that enabled his audience, however large, to hear disti[n]ctly the lowest Sound of his voice."[6] An educated voter was skeptical of Lincoln, saying, "Can't the party raise any better material than that?" But after hearing Lincoln's oration he concluded in astonishment that Lincoln "knew more than all the other candidates put together."[7]

Political candidates found it difficult to appeal to the various norms of civility among the frontiersmen, and difficult to speak about complex issues to a largely illiterate audience. As Ward Hill Lamon later described it, "Every Saturday afternoon the people flocked to the county-seat, to see the candidates, to hear speeches, to discuss prospects, to get drunk and fight."[8] There were generally two types of crowds: one did not always conform to modest public behavior, and the other despised public rowdiness and viewed it as morally reprehensible. Surprisingly, Lincoln experienced more trouble appealing to the latter group than the former. His attraction to Enlightenment ideas spurred an evident religious skepticism, and many people he met suspected him of being an infidel. For example, the Matheny family of Springfield greatly admired Lincoln, but as strong Methodists, they viewed Lincoln as a religious scoffer and could not support him. "Many religious Christian Whigs hated to vote for Lincoln on that account," wrote James Matheny."[9] The qualms about Lincoln's faith, however, did not seem to affect his overall popularity.

Lincoln held that the only proper way to win the esteem of his fellow man would be to earn it, so he embarked on what a friend termed his "hand-shaking campaign," roaming from farm to village across the county to talk with people in their homes and in their fields.[10] People on the frontier resented anyone who smacked of aristocratic privilege, and a politician like Lincoln was a welcome sight. Charles Maltby recalled that the candidate curried favor with "all persons, with the rich or poor, in the stately mansion or log cabin." They found him agreeable and sociable as he asked about their crops, their livestock, their families, their worries, and their hopes.[11] Friend Joseph Gillespie observed that Lincoln held "great faith in the strong sense of Country People and he gave them credit for greater intelligence than most men do."[12] Though more learned, Lincoln did not appear to think himself above them. Those who met him felt, as Maltby put it, that "they had met a friend—one near as a brother."[13]

Lincoln won electoral support using methods that today seem odd. At Island Grove, for example, he encountered some thirty men in a field harvesting their crops. One of the men remarked that they could not vote for a man unless he proved himself. "Boys," said Lincoln, "if that's all, i am shure of your votes." He jumped in and cut more grain than any of them. J. Rowan Herndon, present at that encounter, recalled that the men were so satisfied that "I don't think he Lost a vote in the Croud."[14] At Mechanicsburg Lincoln won admirers by jumping into a free-for-all fight and ending it. On another occasion, Lincoln and John T. Stuart campaigned together at a beef shoot, and in accordance with the common practice of the day, they paid the bill for the beef in order to curry favor with the attendees.[15]

Since Lincoln's initial run for the legislature, the two-party system had become more fully organized both nationally and locally. Politicians now pledged stronger allegiance to chosen political parties. President Jackson remained popular. But, by 1834, six years into his presidency, the anti-Jackson National Republicans formalized more intensely and now called themselves the Whig Party, a name borrowed from the old political party in England that had opposed the king. The Whigs championed Senator Henry Clay as their spokesman, and as a devotee to Clay principles, Lincoln readily embraced the Whig Party platform. According to lawyer Stephen T. Logan, Lincoln stood "as stiff as a man could be in his Whig doctrines."[16] Lincoln gravitated toward the chief members of the Whig Party in Sangamon County, particularly Stuart, who had been elected to the state legislature in his first attempt in 1832 and was now seen as the county's Whig leader. Alongside Stuart, Lincoln would soon garner a reputation as "one of the most devoted Clay whigs" in Illinois.[17]

Stuart, a Kentucky native, possessed many characteristics Lincoln admired. Only a year older than Lincoln, Stuart had come to Illinois to study law and chart a path for himself in politics. He had the benefit of a college education in the classics, a rarity that impressed Lincoln. Their time together during the Black Hawk War cemented their friendship. Many considered Stuart the handsomest man in the state, a courteous and "polished gentleman of the olden school," and of his abilities as a jury lawyer and a politician it was said that "he had no superior in Illinois."[18] Stuart held strongly to his Christian beliefs but admitted that pious people would probably find "my faith is better than my works."[19] Stuart liked and respected his younger counterpart, whom he had taken under his wing, noting that Lincoln "acquired a reputation for candor and honesty," as well as for his ability "in speech-making . . . and thereby acquired the respect and confidence of everybody."[20]

With no political enemies, Lincoln enjoyed popular support from both political camps, particularly in New Salem. Democrats there, "purely out of personal regard for him," offered their support to the candidate, hoping that he might join their cause.[21] The Clary's Grove boys—Jackson men and hard-core Democrats—threatened to fight anyone who dared to publicly criticize their chum Lincoln. "They did this for him simply because he was popular—because he was Lincoln," Logan said.[22] Others joined in. Bowling Green, a staunch Democrat who earlier encouraged Lincoln's first run, warmly endorsed Lincoln's candidacy again in 1834, despite the fact that this time he ran as a Whig.[23]

Sangamon County Democrats did not share the same love for Stuart, whom they wrote off as a Whig stalwart. Green and several county party leaders approached Lincoln in 1834 with a proposition: they would fully support Lincoln, along with their three Democratic candidates, in order to squeeze out Stuart. Lincoln felt it only honorable to alert his friend of the intrigue, which Stuart appreciated. But Stuart believed he was popular enough to withstand the trick and recommended that Lincoln accept the risky proposal. Meanwhile, Stuart's followers directed political arrows toward one particular Democratic candidate, Richard Quinton, hoping to weaken his chances.[24]

New Salem residents spoke to Lincoln about the issues of greatest interest to them. They applauded Lincoln's advocacy for a canal on the Sangamon River connecting New Salem with Petersburg. More important than river navigation to both Democrats and Whigs in New Salem, however, was separating from Sangamon County to form a new county. Located in the far reaches of northwest Sangamon, New Salem residents felt disconnected from the county seat in Springfield. They wanted more autonomy. The villagers made it clear to Lincoln that, if elected, he would be expected to push through legislation that would give them their independence.[25] New Salem resident John Potter relayed that "when Abe ran for the legislature, the time he was elected, Ned Potter and Hugh Armstrong had a pledge from him that he would try to get us cut off and made into a new county." Stuart confirmed that "Lincoln being their local candidate they expected to make him instrumental in bringing this about."[26]

Lincoln's hard campaigning paid off. In the election on August 4, 1834, he won 1,376 votes, second behind the top contender, Democrat John Dawson, who garnered only fourteen votes more. William Carpenter, a farmer and Democrat, polled third. Stuart hung on to finish in the fourth and final spot, winning 1,164 votes. More importantly,

Stuart's counterstrategy—to defeat the Democrat candidate Quinton (who finished just behind Stuart)—worked.[27]

Lincoln's election to the legislature did not stop his debts from dogging him. In the 1830s the Illinois General Assembly met approximately three to four months each year. Legislative service provided supplemental income but could not be a representative's sole occupation. Most legislators enjoyed sustaining employment as lawyers, businessmen, judges, or farmers. Being in the Illinois House, though not a lucrative position, offered Lincoln some relief from his debts. But Stuart offered a brighter opportunity. During the course of their legislative campaign, he encouraged Lincoln to study law with the hope that he might enter the legal profession while in the legislature. Lincoln concurred and, immediately following the 1834 election, Stuart loaned his protégé some of his law books. Lincoln "went at it in good earnest," still engaged in surveying and postmaster duties to pay for room, board, and other expenses.[28] At that time, Lincoln did not even have enough money to buy a set of clothes that would be appropriate for a state legislator. So he sought out New Salem friend Coleman Smoot, who had some financial means. Approaching him, Lincoln asked, "Smoot, did you vote for me?" Smoot responded that he did. Lincoln replied, "Well, that makes you responsible." Lincoln then asked for $200, which Smoot promptly loaned. Lincoln used the funds to pay down some debt, defray traveling expenses for his trip, and purchase the first suit he ever owned.[29]

Basking in electoral victory, Lincoln's pride may have led him to ghostwrite a scathing attack that appeared in the *Beardstown Chronicle* in November 1834. The article, written under the pseudonym of "Sam Hill," questioned the character of Peter Cartwright, who had beat Lincoln in the 1832 legislative race. The minister chose not to run again in 1834 but still dabbled in politics. Charging that Cartwright cared more about politics than the Bible, the article stated, "None has a greater thirst for political distinction than Peter Cartwright." Lincoln had never felt affinity for Cartwright, and in the blistering piece he called the preacher a moral hypocrite and a fool. So vicious were the article's charges that Lincoln's first choice for publication, the *Sangamo Journal,* chose not to publish it.[30] His first exercise in ruthless partisan ghostwriting would be far from his last. For twelve years he would occasionally continue these types of ill-advised attacks until one nearly landed him in a duel with James Shields.

* * *

In late November 1834, the twenty-three-year-old Lincoln hopped on the stagecoach in Springfield to travel seventy-five miles southward to the state capital in Vandalia. Three of his fellow representatives from Sangamon County accompanied him. The slow and at times uncomfortable ride, which consumed nearly two days, ended in front of the post office in Vandalia, a town of some eight hundred inhabitants. Perched on a bluff overlooking the Kaskaskia River, the state capital was at the junction of two important roads: the well-traveled "National Road" from Cumberland, Maryland, to Vandalia, and the north-south trace that connected Shawneetown to Springfield and points north. Smaller than Springfield, Vandalia had existed for only fifteen years. However, it bustled with "busy, buzzing, bargaining" activity, noted one observer.[31] The state legislature, the state supreme court, and a federal court conducted business in the town. Government workers, prominent lawyers, capitalists, and lobbyists converged there. Many men brought their wives and daughters, and rounds of parties and dances enlivened the legislative sessions. The taverns brimmed with hard drinks, loud laughs, and hearty conversation.[32]

Though it was a lively town, those who had seen grander state capitals in the East found Vandalia disappointing. "The public edifices are very inconsiderable," wrote one visitor in the 1830s, noting the "ordinary structure of brick for legislative purposes."[33] The Presbyterian church, the stone bank building, and a few "lesser buildings for purposes of worship and education," were all that indicated the frontier town was a capital city. Even the important National Road leading into town remained only partially constructed. Surrounding timberland hid the town; Vandalia certainly could not claim to be a beacon. The same traveler noted that "legislators who assembled in session at this place sought their way through the neighbouring prairies as the mariner steers over the trackless ocean."[34]

Visitors found few choice accommodations in town. Some legislators lodged at the Vandalia Inn or the four other hotels, where they might be lucky enough to indulge in wine and liquor. Some found boarding rooms above private residences. Stuart and Lincoln roomed together probably in the second story of a frame house, along with several other assemblymen in adjacent rooms. Stuart put a positive spin on the lodging, saying, "The members were very much thrown together and learned to know each other very well. We had a very pleasant time." However, he lamented that because Vandalia remained small, it offered little in the way of fine dining. He later recalled, "A piece of fat pork was a luxury in those days." Already in 1834 talk ensued about relocating the capital, since legislators "had such a longing for something civilized," Stuart recollected.[35]

One of only two brick buildings in Vandalia, the two-story statehouse provided chambers on the first floor for the House members and on the second floor for the Senate, plus a room for the Illinois Supreme Court. Immediately after the original capitol burned in 1823, workers built another. But after ten years that building had already fallen into such disrepair that crashes of falling plaster sometimes interrupted the sessions. Light could be seen through cracks, one wall bulged out several inches, and the upstairs Senate floor sunk toward the center. House members were seated in uncomfortable chairs at long, unadorned tables, each accommodating three people. Candles in tall holders provided the chamber's dim light. A fireplace and a stove provided pockets of warmth. Spittoons lined the room. What few glimpses of prestige the building offered were provided by men of some substance who might be donned in smart apparel, or ladies in fashionable dresses who assembled in the gallery to watch the proceedings. The building's exterior did not impress either. The largest public building in Illinois at the time, its rustic appearance harkened back to a rural frontier of days gone by.[36]

Lincoln took his seat as a state representative in the Ninth Illinois General Assembly on December 1, 1834. Lincoln's lanky, six-foot-four frame fascinated his colleagues, but his height posed problems. The desks were built for smaller men, and Lincoln had to sit sideways because his legs were so long. When he stood to speak, observers teased that it took him five minutes to get his legs together to straighten up. Once when Lincoln was asked how long a man's legs should be, he humorously responded: "Long enough to reach from his body to the ground."[37]

Many of his new colleagues had a great deal of political training and experience. The state senate had twenty-six members, including Benjamin Bond, son of the state's first governor, Shadrach Bond; Cyrus Edwards, of the prominent and wealthy Edwards family; William Gatewood, first commissioner of the Gallatin Salines; John W. Vance, a wealthy salt manufacturer from Vermilion County; Thomas Mather, a businessman soon to be president of the state bank; and Dr. Conrad Will, a delegate of the first state Constitutional Convention. Fifty-four other legislators joined Lincoln in the Illinois House of Representatives for the 1834–35 session. Among Lincoln's colleagues in the House were Robert Blackwell, who started one of the first printing presses in the state; General William McHenry, veteran of the War of 1812 and member of the General Assembly since Illinois achieved statehood in 1818; and Thomas J. Owen, later the first mayor of Chicago. More than a dozen had served as officers in the Black Hawk War. More than half the members were farmers, about a fourth were lawyers, and the remainder were merchants or of other professions. The overwhelming majority of the legislators were, like Lincoln, born in the South. In fact, only one member of the entire assembly, Representative John Whiteside of Monroe County, could claim to be a native-born Illinoisan.[38]

While the state's Ninth General Assembly boasted some prestige, many entered their names as representatives for the first time. Thirty-six of the fifty-four House members in 1834 were freshmen, and only one—William McHenry—had served longer than three terms. The state legislature at that time experienced a rapid turnover rate. A candidate needed only to make himself agreeable enough to the people to get elected. Thus many ran and won, then moved on to other positions or lost their re-election bids when they ignored constituent wishes.[39] As with Lincoln, some felt a thirst for politics and public service; for others, the legislature served as a step on the ladder of advancement to higher office. Regardless of motivation, Thomas

Ford, who later became governor, concluded that many legislators shrewdly "cultivated the arts of popularity" in order to be elected.[40]

In addition to including many first-timers, this assembly exhibited relative youthfulness. The twenty-five-year-old Lincoln, the second youngest of all the representatives, joined a squad of other members in their twenties or early thirties.[41] Among them were Jesse Dubois, William Fithian, and John Stuart, all of whom would become instrumental in Lincoln's political rise. Lincoln forged particular immediate collegiality with Lawrence County representative Dubois, as they shared many similar views and aspirations. Described as a slim, handsome young man "with the elegant manners of a Frenchman," the fiery Dubois gravitated to the ambitious Lincoln.[42] He gave a first impression of Lincoln's appearance far more complimentary than most. He gazed upon the Sangamon representative as a "very decent looking fellow," appropriately dressed in loose trousers, the accepted fashion among the Whigs.[43] Dubois became a fast friend and would be a loyal supporter of Lincoln for years to come.

Democrats, who controlled the legislature, elected James Semple of Madison County as House Speaker. Semple, a Kentucky native and veteran of the Black Hawk War, had a reputation for being capable but domineering.[44] John T. Stuart won the vote of his party to be the Whig floor leader, a prestigious position granting him party leadership in the House. After the leadership was established, committee assignments were doled out. Some members were appointed to two or three committees. Lincoln, as a freshman member of the opposition party, drew only one assignment: the Committee on Public Accounts and Expenditures.[45]

A spirit of hope regarding the state's future filled the General Assembly in 1834–35. Illinois, a state for sixteen years at that point, had witnessed rapid growth. Its population exceeded two hundred thousand, remaining heaviest toward the southern end of the state but growing especially in the state's northern reaches in young cities such as Chicago.[46] A traveler to Illinois in the 1830s expressed astonishment at the rapid increase in the state's population, noting, "To this region the speculator is attracted by the increasing value of property; the politician anticipates the time when, through the ballot-box, the West shall rule; . . . the direction of our government will shortly be in the hands of the people of the West."[47] Chicago, more than any other town in Illinois, witnessed an explosion in wealth and population in the 1830s. A natural harbor for ships, it held promise. Agriculture provided the state's chief occupation, and farmers shipped a great amount to meet the demand from the East Coast. The same traveler also wrote, "The state of Illinois has probably the finest body of fertile land of any state in the Union, and the opportunities for speculation are numerous. . . . Fertile soil is already producing abundant agriculture twice as much as out East."[48]

Not only did Illinois witness a population explosion in the 1830s, but the state also saw a great accumulation of wealth. Land speculators rushed into Illinois and bought up land only to sell it at much higher prices to new emigrants. Consequently, because the state had sold so much land, the state treasury stood debt free in 1834, and all demands were paid with cash. With Illinois's rapid growth, transportation remained a high priority. The General Assembly considered it their responsibility to continue that growth. Special acts of the legislature were needed to charter towns, open roads, build bridges, incorporate banks, and establish educational institutions.[49] As early as 1830, Illinois governor John Reynolds encouraged the state to release some of its revenue to build up the state's infrastructure. "There cannot be an appropriation of money within the exercise of your legislative powers," he said, "that will be more richly paid to the citizens than that for the internal improvement of the country."[50]

His gubernatorial successor, Joseph Duncan, echoed Reynolds's plea in 1834. Just before the legislature opened its session, Duncan said, "Our state is comparatively in its infancy, and if roads, trackways, railroads, and canals, are now laid out . . . with very little expense," he predicted, lands would increase in value.[51] With that urgency, the push for new roads, canals, and railroads reached a fever pitch. Private companies who could build railroads submitted grand plans. Many imagined the possibility that all corners of the state could be connected by rail, that every river could be widened and deepened, and that a great canal system could be realized. This fervor for internal improvements dominated the legislative agenda in the 1834–35 session.[52]

In just his fifth day in the legislature Lincoln recorded his first act: his intention to propose a bill. In accordance with standard procedure, legislators submitted to the House speaker their intention to propose bills. Bills received a first reading but were not automatically forwarded to appropriate committees as legislation is today. Voice voting would immediately take place to accept a bill for a second reading—usually not held the same day unless rules were suspended—or to send to committee to amend the bill, or to table it. If requested by legislators, the "yeas" and "nays" of those votes might be recorded in the *House Journal*. If no objection occurred after a bill's second reading, it would be "engrossed"—meaning it would be ordered to a third reading pending any further amendments and concurrence on the bill from the state senate.[53] Later in the session Lincoln would propose a measure mandating that no amendments could be added to a bill after its third reading, so as not to prolong the process. The House defeated the measure; however, the rule Lincoln suggested is now common practice in the Illinois House.[54]

In his communication to the speaker on his first bill, Lincoln wrote, "On monday next or some day thereafter I shall ask leave to introduce a bill entitled to limit the jurisdiction of justices of the peace."[55] Lincoln's bill held a distinct purpose—to give the many impoverished and defenseless settlers a judge in their locality to try their civil lawsuits. Lincoln believed that limiting judges' authority to localized regions would give greater legal advantage to poor residents. He knew from his own experience that had he the benefit of a judge who personally knew him when faced with his own debts, he might have received a more agreeable settlement.[56] Unfortunately, Lincoln's very first bill got lost in the slew of other bills and never saw the light of day. A week later, he again took the floor for his second bill. "Mr. Speaker," he announced, "I now give notice that Thursday next, or some day thereafter I shall ask leave to introduce a bill entitled an act to authorize Samuel Musick to build a toll bridge across Salt Creek in Sangamon County."[57] That second bill received a more favorable result, eventually winning passage.[58]

Lincoln attended the session, but as a first-termer maintained a low profile, preferring to listen and observe. Sitting in his seat near the corner of the chamber, he took note of the finer points of parliamentary procedure. He saw the often mundane legislative business, such as appropriating $2.50 to fix the stoves in the statehouse. He watched as legislators crafted bills designed to win the support of likeminded legislators and curry favor with voters back home. He also noted the art of logrolling—the bartering and trading of favors and votes on legislation between representatives. Lincoln observed legislators jockeying for rank and their ceaseless push to win offices for their friends who got them elected. He witnessed in amazement as more than a hundred individuals converged to apply for the single position of doorkeeper of the House.[59] These political activities prompted representative William Fithian to write in frustration, "We have been here now two weeks and as yet so far as I can judge, not one measure has been adopted for the benefit of the people of Illinois."[60]

Lincoln keenly detected the major players, marveling at how popularity and personal influence determined success in the realm of politics. Though quiet at first, he slowly joined in and acquainted himself closely with other members, especially with those who he felt might be of political advantage to him.[61]

In addition to learning all he could about the political process, Lincoln explored Vandalia. Occasionally he slipped out of the legislative chamber to watch the Illinois Supreme Court in action. In the evenings, he might take in the lively political talk in the taverns. He sporadically attended the popular cotillions and parties such as those held at the Vandalia Hotel, the hot spot for social events. Many legislators indulged in excess drinking and gambling, which prompted one citizen to wish that professing Christians would take greater precaution in the caliber of those they elect to the legislature.[62] Lincoln, however, preferred not to engage in such activities. He also chose not to dance with the women at evening socials, as his rough manners and unkempt appearance did him no favors. On one occasion, he finally mustered the courage to ask a particular woman to dance, but in his awkwardness stepped on her dress and tore it. She graciously forgave the apologetic and embarrassed Lincoln.[63]

In the male world of politics, however, Lincoln excelled at developing relationships. He especially spent a great deal of time with

Stuart. One acquaintance noted of the pair that "socially and politically they seemed inseparable."[64] In day-to-day House activity, Stuart overshadowed Lincoln. The junior representative hung under the Whig floor leader's wing, watching and learning from his slightly more experienced mentor. Their lodging served as an unofficial headquarters for the Whigs. Fellow legislators seeking favors, pushing legislation, or simply debating issues and ideas visited Stuart and Lincoln's room. Stuart would introduce his protégé, and young Lincoln, with his face beaming, would offer a hearty handshake in his huge, coarse, but welcoming hands. The introductions Stuart provided his understudy were instrumental in Lincoln's forging alliances and friendships in the legislature.[65]

Lincoln and Stuart largely acted in concert during the session. Proving he was his own man, however, Lincoln voted independently of Stuart on twenty-six out of a 126 votes. Though Lincoln introduced few bills on his own, he wrote and provided influence on others legislators' bills, including Stuart's. Stuart increasingly relied on Lincoln, perhaps grooming him for advancement. The demands of serving as Whig floor leader and serving on multiple committees compelled Stuart to be absent from debates in the House chamber, and when he was unavailable, Stuart routinely asked Lincoln to speak for him on the floor. On no occasion in roll call votes were both Stuart and Lincoln absent.[66] Stuart often allowed Lincoln to handle his political "horse-trading" for him. Stuart became so known for his politicking that he earned the nickname "Jerry Sly."[67] But Stuart witnessed that as Lincoln gained more experience and more knowledge "of the tricks &c of men," he still refused to be bribed in exchange for votes.[68]

While Lincoln would not be bought off, he would participate with Stuart in vote trading. Once representative Sidney Breese approached Stuart and Lincoln with the desire to build a railroad on the state's credit. The Sangamon County duo was happy to support railroad ventures, as were many in the legislature. Stuart and Lincoln concurrently wished to name certain friends canal commissioners. So they signed on to the deal to support Breese's measure, and Breese, in turn, helped obtain the desired appointments.[69]

As Lincoln learned the art of politicking, he became aware of one highly anticipated issue among his colleagues: the construction of the Illinois and Michigan Canal. The positive results a canal could yield were many. The Illinois River meandered through the heart of Illinois. Opening the river further might allow for larger boat transportation, and constructing a canal would connect the Mississippi River to Lake Michigan and the other Great Lakes. Thus, the proposed canal would allow Illinois to serve as a continuous transportation corridor both from the Mississippi River to the Gulf of Mexico and from the Great Lakes to the port cities in the eastern United States. The Illinois and Michigan Canal would ensure that Illinois products had easy access to markets throughout the world.

The first American canal project was the much-celebrated Erie Canal. In 1817 New York governor DeWitt Clinton envisioned a canal system that would connect the city of Buffalo—situated on the edge of Lake Erie in western New York—with New York City, providing access to the Atlantic Ocean. Clinton and the canal proponents argued that easy east-west navigation from the Great Lakes to the Atlantic would guarantee New York as a trade hub. Despite heavy criticism over the enormous cost of the project, the New York legislature agreed to Clinton's proposal and invested $7 million—a hefty sum at that time. Completed in 1825, the Erie Canal surpassed the expectations of even its advocates. The populations of both Buffalo and New York City exploded, and the latter city rapidly surpassed Philadelphia, Boston, and other East Coast cities as an international trade port. Residually, the state's wealth grew. Many people in Illinois believed that a canal that could connect Illinois to the waterways of the mighty Mississippi and the Great Lakes would result in a similar leap in population and prosperity for the state.[70]

As early as 1821, Sangamon County state senator George Forquer, chairman of the Committee on Internal Improvements, made a report to the Illinois legislature in favor of a loan of a half-million dollars on state credit to begin the canal. The matter passed both houses of the General Assembly that session, and the legislature ordered a survey of the region from LaSalle to Lake Michigan. But the development of railroads left the canal plan in question. By 1832, the General Assembly considered construction of railroads as an alternative to the Illinois and Michigan Canal and even approved a charter to build a railroad from the Illinois River to Lake Michigan instead of digging a canal. However, they quickly concluded, very much as Lincoln had in his 1832 campaign platform, that railroads might be too costly. So the legislature again turned back to the canal. But not all were willing to abandon the dream of railroads, and that session became mired in a debate over building a railroad versus building a canal.[71]

In the 1834–35 session, the state legislature recommitted itself to the Illinois and Michigan Canal project. With little opposition, legislators authorized a loan of $500,000 to support state bond sales toward the canal, implying it would be just the beginning of years of support. Lincoln had earlier held that federal money raised through the sale of public lands should provide the bulk of funding for internal state improvements. In this case, however, he had no opposition to the state's paying for the project.[72] A few legislators dissented, arguing that only private financing should support the canal, but most agreed that private companies should not control public works. Thus, the legislature approved the canal funding on the credit and faith of the state.[73]

Not only did Lincoln give wholehearted backing to public financing of the canal, but his support for the Illinois and Michigan Canal proved vital to the bill. State representative Gurdon Hubbard of Vermilion County had pushed for passage of the canal in the 1832 term to no avail. Now out of the legislature, Hubbard lobbied tirelessly for the project in 1834, identifying legislators he considered friendly to the cause and whose merit and influence might help guide it through the channels of legislative procedure. Hubbard found Lincoln and begged his aid to carry the project with his colleagues in the legislature. Lincoln embraced and pursued the effort. "We were thrown much together," Hubbard recalled, "our intimacy increasing." "Indeed, I very much doubt if the bill could have passed as easily as it did without his valuable help."[74] But Lincoln did not award himself praise. After passage of the bill, Lincoln acclaimed men such as Hubbard who had pushed the canal plan in previous sessions. He dedicated passage of the bill "to the untiring zeal of Mr. Stuart," whose "high minded and honorable way" had secured "the accomplishment of this great work."[75]

Soon Lincoln found that another important and controversial matter took center stage within the legislature during his first session in office: the rechartering of the Bank of Illinois. The legislature had not intended to take up the issue, but heated wrangling between President Jackson and Congress over the Second Bank of the United States—the country's national bank—sent the banking issue rippling into state governments as well.

In 1816 Congress had chartered the Second Bank of the United States in Philadelphia for a twenty-year cycle. The national bank handled all financial transactions for the federal government, established a stable currency system for the country, and regulated the credit issued by banking institutions. Since the bank assumed functions for the U.S. Treasury, it was accountable to both Congress and the Treasury Department. The ownership of the bank rested largely with thousands of private stockholders. Although the federal government remained the single largest stockholder with 20 percent ownership, a few hundred wealthy investors held the bulk of the stocks. Congress would need to recharter the Second Bank and its twenty-five subsidiary banks by 1836 for it to continue. President Andrew Jackson, who considered the national bank a corrupt institution used by rich bankers and politicians to control the credit and wealth of the country, made it an issue in his re-election in 1832. Securing a victory, he saw his re-election as a mandate to kill the bank, and, in 1833, by executive order, directed that funds be removed from the bank's control. Thus he engaged in a battle with Congress, particularly with bank president Nicholas Biddle, and one of the bank's congressional supporters, senator Henry Clay.[76]

Across the country, state legislatures lined up behind their party allegiances. Democrats in the Illinois legislature, led by representative J. B. Thomas of Madison, introduced a resolution of support for Jackson, calling the national bank system "a soulless corporation."[77] Lincoln naturally voted with the Whigs against Thomas's resolution and in support of the bank.[78]

State banks had also witnessed their share of problems. Even before becoming a state, the Illinois territorial legislature in 1817 authorized the formation of the first Bank of Illinois, with locations in Shawneetown, Edwardsville, and Kaskaskia. By 1821, residual effects from the economic panic of 1819 and unanswered questions over how to handle the public money caused the Bank of Illinois to fail. As a result, the state's residents generally disdained a state banking system. When the 1834 session opened, the legislature did not intend to renew the state bank. But Jackson's threat to remove funds from the Second Bank of the United States reopened the state bank debate. Democrats erroneously believed that Whigs would be opposed to the idea of a state bank since they were so supportive of the national bank. However, the Whigs and some Democrats agreed that a state banking system of some sort should be formulated when the national bank ceased to exist. After all, there were state funds within the control of the national bank, and a replacement bank in which to place state funds would be needed if the national bank closed. The argument held that a regulated banking system would provide for sound currency. Also, profits from a state banking system could pay for state projects, such as internal improvements. In keeping with his economic tenets, Lincoln believed that a state bank, properly operated, could allow the surplus capital of the rich to be invested and available to the industrious poor person so he might get ahead. Thus a favorable concert of Whigs and Democrats in both chambers of the legislature, Lincoln included, approved the removal of state funds from the national bank and created state bank charters. The new Bank of Illinois headquarters would be in Springfield, in the center of the state, with branches in Vandalia, Alton, Jacksonville, and other larger Illinois towns. The same banking bill called for the reopening of the Bank of Illinois at Shawneetown.[79]

After supporting a new state bank, Lincoln encountered another issue of key importance to the legislature: the sale of public lands in Illinois. The federal government had long laid claim to unpopulated lands in the "Old Northwest." As pioneers in the 1830s continued moving into Illinois from the southern and eastern parts of the United States, the federal government began selling land to speculators and private individuals and pocketing the revenues. By 1837, speculators actually owned the majority of the land in Illinois.[80] State governments received no profits from such sales within their borders. Early in the 1834 session, Lincoln introduced a resolution urging congressmen to pass a law entitling the state to 20 percent of the amount paid to the U.S. Treasury for sales of Illinois public lands. Money flowing into the state, Lincoln reasoned, would offset the expense of state projects such that costs "would be a burden of no sort of consequence."[81] The measure sailed through both houses of the state legislature, but not surprisingly, Congress never took action on it.[82]

Compared with other state representatives, Lincoln presented relatively few bills in his freshman session. Those he did submit for consideration reflected his pledge to represent the wishes of his constituents. His toll-bridge bill and road-construction bill both passed. True to his campaign pledge, he proposed "an act to improve the navigation of the Sangamon River," which passed the House. On behalf of his New Salem constituents, Lincoln presented a petition to the House to carve out a new county from Sangamon, Morgan, and Tazewell counties. However, time ran out in the session, and the legislature took no action on that matter.[83] The fact, however, that he fulfilled these campaign pledges to his constituents would serve him well in his next election.

Lincoln was particularly interested in some of the other issues the General Assembly took up during the 1834–35 session, although he did not campaign on them. One issue important to him was the establishment of a school system in Illinois. Many children in the state did not attend any school at all. Before the start of the 1834 legislative session, Sangamon County elected Lincoln to represent them at a state education convention in Vandalia. Vowing to educate every child in the state, Governor Joseph Duncan affirmed the need to adopt a statewide public education system, informing the legislature that "education under all forms of government, constitutes the first principle of human happiness; and especially, it is important in a country, where the sovereignty is vested in the people." Submitting a bill to the legislature in 1835, the governor continued, "General education is the only means by which the rich and the poor can be placed upon the same level," a sentiment Lincoln most certainly embraced.[84] The question of how to fund the common school system in Illinois, however, remained unanswered. Should the state rely upon money borrowed from the federal government for schools, or should taxes be raised to pay for education? The governor gave no recommendations either way, and the legislature took no further action. In a related measure, Lincoln supported an effort to provide for education of orphan children, but it met defeat in the House.[85]

Another issue that would have long-term implications for Lincoln was the need to reorganize the state circuit court system, which had been established according to the 1818 Illinois Constitution. Population shifts made the redrawing of circuit boundaries necessary. Five circuits were thus created with allowances to carve additional circuit districts as population increased. Under this system Lincoln would begin his circuit-riding law practice a few years later. For judge of the first judicial district, which included Sangamon County, the legislature elected—with Lincoln's vote among the majority— Stephen T. Logan, who would later become Lincoln's law partner. Not only did they elect judges at that time, but the legislature also elected positions in state government including state attorneys, state auditor, state treasurer, state attorney general, and state printer. The business of appointments sometimes seemed nonsensical to Lincoln, such as when the legislature attempted to appoint a new surveyor in Schuyler County where someone already occupied the position. During a speech on the House floor, Lincoln sardonically applauded the move, quipping that "if the old surveyor should . . . conclude to die, there would be a new one ready made without troubling the legislature."[86]

That speech, near the end of the session, won Lincoln some attention. Representatives unfamiliar with him except by name and those who had not heard him speak at the podium were struck by his ability to apply wit and simple logical arguments to issues. Speaker Semple had taken notice of Lincoln's abilities, naming Lincoln to at least ten special committees during the course of the session.[87] While the Sangamon County legislator had not won any fame, forwarded any major proposals, or succeeded in addressing his campaign platform of interest rates and county division in his first legislative session, he gained the attention of his colleagues. "Before that first session of 1834 [and early 1835] was over, Lincoln was already . . . prominent," Dubois recalled, concluding that he was "more than an ordinary man."[88]

Lincoln's record proves his eagerness for prominence. Though not in the forefront of legislation, he was an active participant. Of 1,138 roll call votes on bills and procedural matters, Lincoln missed only eight votes, compared to the average of all members at thirteen.[89] Beyond that, he had acted behind the scenes as the political correspondent for the *Sangamo Journal,* sending to the newspaper periodic updates on various bills before the legislature.[90] This taste for public service in the first few months of his legislative career emboldened young Lincoln. The quest for distinction, in the words of William Herndon, "whetted his appetite for further honors."[91] Upon his return to New Salem, a resident noticed more confidence in the legislator for his abilities, remarking, "Mr. Lincoln improved rapidly in Mind & Manners after his return from Vandalia his first Session in the Legislature."[92]

Vandalia State House. The statehouse in Vandalia served as the capitol from its construction in 1836 to 1839, when the capital was moved to Springfield. Courtesy of Fayette County Museum.

LAWYER, LEGISLATOR,
LOGROLLER, LEADER

On February 13, 1835, the General Assembly adjourned. Lincoln returned home to his surveying and postmaster duties. He longed to tear open the law books Stuart had loaned him so that alongside politics he might prepare for a career in law. For his two-and-a-half month legislative session, he pocketed a salary of three dollars a day—$258 total, including traveling expenses.[1] Though his income was meager, it provided enough to allow him to begin repaying his debt.

Finances aside, with a new sense of direction, Lincoln decided to broaden his social life. A young woman in New Salem had caught his fancy: Ann Rutledge, the twenty-two-year-old daughter of tavern owner James Rutledge. While Ann was purportedly pledged to marry another man and the nature of Lincoln's relationship with her is not known, the two engaged in laughter and hearty conversation, read books together, and enjoyed strolls through the village. However deep their intimacy, when Ann tragically died of typhoid in August of 1835, Lincoln plunged into severe depression.[2]

Lincoln had not managed to recover from Rutledge's death when Governor Joseph Duncan called a special session of the General Assembly to begin in December 1835. The session's goals were to expedite work toward construction of the Illinois and Michigan Canal, to fund the state bank, and to reapportion the state's legislative districts based on the 1835 state census.[3] Still absorbed in melancholy, Lincoln promptly left New Salem and again traversed the countryside with the Sangamon County delegation southward to Vandalia.

As Lincoln took his seat in the legislature, national politics grabbed center stage. Earlier in the year President Andrew Jackson had announced that he would not run again in 1836. Jackson had formed a broad coalition of Democrats during his two terms, but no one else in his party held the consensus as well as he did. In an effort to preclude a dissolution of the party, the Democrats held a national convention in Baltimore in May 1835. They nominated vice president Martin Van Buren as their presidential candidate. Van Buren could share credit for building the Democratic Party, and he held most of Jackson's views, but his dignified dress and manners made him appear stuffy, aristocratic, and not as correspondent with the common man as Jackson. Hence, Van Buren did not enjoy widespread popularity in Illinois. As a way to build party momentum and keep the party faithful solidified behind Van Buren, Democrats in Illinois decided to hold the state's first political nominating convention. Led by attorney Stephen A. Douglas from Jacksonville, Democrats staged their convention in the statehouse in Vandalia on December 5, 1835, the same day the legislature convened.[4]

When partisan politics appeared, Lincoln toed the party line. Two days after the Democratic state convention, he joined the Whigs in denouncing the very idea of a party convention, stating that taking the selection of candidates out of voters' hands "ought not to be tolerated in a republican government."[5] Not to be outhustled, the Democrats, in turn, proposed a resolution extolling the Democratic presidential ticket for 1836 with Van Buren as their choice. As a faithful Whig, Lincoln voted against that resolution.[6] More partisan plays followed. When the Democrats in the state legislature called for a removal of the Congressional censure against President Jackson, the Whigs, including Lincoln, voted against it.[7]

Despite strong partisan impulses, Lincoln did not hesitate to reach across the aisle to befriend members of the opposition party. During this session he became acquainted with fellow representative Orlando B. Ficklin, a Democrat from Wabash County. Only a few months apart in age, they both hailed from Kentucky, were consummate storytellers, and had served as officers in the Black Hawk War. From the moment they met, Ficklin found Lincoln appealing. In Ficklin's words a "friendship then commenced which remained unbroken by political differences or personal interests or otherwise," for the rest of their lives.[8]

When Ficklin and Lincoln joined their legislative colleagues in early December 1835, Governor Duncan addressed the General Assembly with another call for internal improvements. "When we see the canal boat and the locomotive bearing with seeming triumph, the rich productions of the interior to the rivers, lakes, and ocean, what patriotic bosom," he asked, "does not beat high with laudable ambition to give Illinois her full share of those advantages?" Such building projects, he foretold, would greatly increase the state's wealth and prosperity. But while urging "the most liberal support" of all such measures of internal improvements, he cautioned the legislature to avoid debt by leaving the funding and construction of all such projects, when possible, up to individual enterprise and to not have the state assume the financial burden.[9]

Lincoln wrote to Thomas Nance at New Salem in mid-December 1835 of his frustration that, despite the governor's agenda for the special session, "There is but little of interest doing in the Legislature as yet."[10] He did not have to wait long. The legislature soon introduced a flurry of bills. All told, the House presented 139 bills and the Senate introduced 106 in the short session. Road and railroad requests comprised the overwhelming majority of the bills, with a few related to bridges and canals.[11] Of the seventeen railroad charters granted, all were directed to be privately financed.[12] The legislature also moved to incorporate the Illinois Central Railroad, which would become an essential conduit for transportation for years to come.

Both houses of the General Assembly crafted and recrafted legislation on the all-important Illinois and Michigan Canal. As the project gained momentum, legislators attempted to attach pet requests to it, and Lincoln was among them. He submitted a proposal to incorporate the Beardstown and Sangamon Canal, with its eastern terminus in Huron near New Salem, into the legislation. The project would certainly aid Lincoln's home community, and while there is every reason to believe that the benefit of his constituents and not self-serving reasons motivated his push for the projects, he would have gained personally from the endeavor. Prior to this, Lincoln had urged the citizens of Petersburg and New Salem to purchase shares of stock for a canal and did so himself. He also acquired some land near the Beardstown and Sangamon Canal's boundary—possibly as payment for surveying.[13] Soon after the session ended, he would buy more shares of stock in the local canal venture.[14]

As a member of the Committee on Public Accounts and Expenditures, Lincoln labored to determine the most prudent manner for the state to dole out its money and to defray increasing expenses. The lack of prestige associated with the committee did not seem to bother him. He pored over the numbers, even missing three days of roll-call votes to construct the committee's report. He learned that the cost of running the General Assembly would be the state's biggest expense, followed by interest on loans, then funds for public projects and incidentals. Other budget items included salaries for the governor, treasurer, secretary of state, Supreme Court judges, circuit judges, state attorneys, state penitentiary wardens, the public printer for state documents, and the manager of the salines.[15] Lincoln also gave a laudable nod toward government transparency when he moved to "enquire into the expediency of authorizeing the publishing of the State laws, of a general nature, in the public Newspapers."[16]

In addition to his work on the committee, Lincoln made a motion regarding Governor Duncan's request that the legislature address redistricting according to the 1835 state census. The state's population had exploded by nearly 60 percent from 1830 to 1835. The number of residents increased from 157,445 residents to 269,974.[17] Legislative leaders therefore resolved to enlarge the number of representatives in the House. At that time, each member represented approximately a thousand residents.[18] Lincoln moved to keep the number of representatives the same, and increase to eighty-five hundred the number of constituents per representative. The majority of his colleagues did not subscribe to Lincoln's alternative option and defeated his motion.[19]

Lincoln also made a popular move. The General Assembly attempted to aid struggling Illinoisans who had incurred debt under insolvent state banks, and Lincoln offered measures to provide relief to those debtors. He also worked to ensure that before any reserve stock be given to the new Bank of Illinois, the bank must be obligated to pay off the outstanding $100,000 "Wiggins loan" given in 1831 by the state to prop up the bank. Even the Democratic newspaper in Springfield praised Lincoln for this action.[20]

Though Lincoln may have appreciated praise in the local Democratic newspaper, he cheered efforts to minimize the power of the Democrats where he could. The General Assembly was tasked with the constitutional duty of selecting the state's U.S. senators, and such an occasion arose when U.S. senator Elias Kane died during the special session. Several candidates emerged including House Speaker James Semple. Lincoln and Semple had been warm to each other, but Semple's Democratic Party proclivities turned Lincoln away. Lincoln voted instead for Black Hawk War hero William Lee Davidson Ewing, a man prepossessed of "considerable notoriety, popularity, and talents" who attracted attention through his elegant fashion.[21] This was the same Ewing whom Lincoln had first witnessed giving a stump speech shortly after his 1830 arrival in Illinois. Ewing had won that state representative race and was immediately elected House Speaker. Two years later he ran for the Illinois Senate and won. After the governor died, Ewing served for fifteen days as the state's chief executive. Although the ambitious Ewing possessed a dark side—he once threw a chair at a legislator during a debate, and another time he stabbed a man he disagreed with—his experience and his immense popularity cast him as a notable figure in Illinois politics.[22] Ewing did not declare a party, and Lincoln would likely have lent his support to a Whig candidate had one vied for the position. The legislature awarded Ewing the U.S. Senate seat, and Lincoln's vote against Semple cost him his favor with the speaker. But that bothered the partisan Lincoln little. He cheered efforts to minimize the power of the Democrats where he could. Writing an account of the Senate election for the *Sangamo Journal* under the pen name "Our Correspondent," Lincoln compared the chipping away at the Democrats' power to shooting and killing "large fowls."[23]

Lincoln's instincts to side with small farmers led him to vote against a bill the legislature passed that may at the time have seemed insignificant but would later raise a firestorm. Lincoln moved to open discussion on the "little bull law," a bill that put strict limits on cattle ownership and breeding. The bill required young bulls to be penned up, assessing steep fines on owners of stray bulls that escaped their enclosures and bred with neighbors' cows. Farmers also had to have their bulls inspected or rent purebred bulls for breeding for a steep fee of thirty dollars. Assessed fines and fees would be distributed in each county as award prizes for best purebred bulls and cows. Lincoln rightly suspected that the common voter would find the bill discriminatory.[24]

The day before the General Assembly adjourned in February 1836, Lincoln submitted a petition similar to one in the previous session on behalf of the citizens of Sangamon, Morgan, and Tazewell "praying the organization of a new county out of said counties."[25] He had delayed his petition until the session's end so that more pressing legislation could be tackled. He also did not foresee its successful passage but wanted to give the impression that he had tried. Not surprisingly, the conclusion of the session derailed any chance of the measure's success.

Once again, Lincoln had faithfully represented his constituents through his dedication to attendance. He missed only seven of 121 roll call votes during the special session.[26] Pocketing his $162 in pay, Lincoln returned to New Salem. His service as postmaster ended when the New Salem post office closed, and he collected his final seventy-five dollars for the previous year's work. To augment his personal finances, he continued as assistant Sangamon County surveyor.[27]

Prospects were bright for Lincoln, and he had every reason to be optimistic about his future. In March 1836, the Sangamon Circuit Court certified him as a person of good moral character. This procedure was the required first step for anyone wishing to gain admission to the bar. That same month, looking forward to advancement in the state legislature, Lincoln joined Robert L. Wilson and Ninian W. Edwards—son of the former Illinois territorial governor—in announcing candidacies for another term in the legislature. Stuart announced that he would now run for Congress.[28] While that was not surprising to Lincoln, it would be very different after having had his mentor constantly by his side in the first term. With William Carpenter garnering a lucrative office as postmaster in Springfield, another seat opened. Thanks to the reapportionment passed in the previous legislative session, Sangamon County was now eligible for seven state representatives, an increase of three and the highest number of any county in the state. In contrast, the state's uneven population left northern Illinois state representative John Hamlin with six counties to represent.[29]

Uncertain who the legislative candidates would be, the *Sangamo Journal* in June 1836 invited all candidates running for the state legislature to "show their hands." Lincoln responded to the *Journal*, writing, "Agreed. Here's mine!"[30] He then proceeded to outline his campaign principles in a statement decidedly more philosophical than his 1832 announcement. He stated, "I go for all sharing the privileges of the government, who assist in bearing its burthens. Consequently I go for admitting all whites to the right of suffrage, who pay taxes or bear arms, (by no means excluding females.)"[31] In the 1834–35 session, Lincoln supported a successful move to ensure that the right to vote extended to all white males of the age of twenty-one years, and not just to those "who hold real estate."[32] In doing so, he more fully embraced the tenets of Jacksonians. However, not many Jacksonians shared Lincoln's belief in women's suffrage—that democracy and equality should be shared by all—regardless of gender, social status, or race. These ideals he would hold dear for the rest of his years.

Lincoln went on to remind voters that he took seriously his role as their representative. To that end he wrote, "I shall be governed by their will, on all subjects upon which I have the means of knowing what their will is; and upon all others, I shall do what my own judgment teaches me will best advance their interests." Where Lincoln addressed specific issues in his announcement, he did so succinctly. "I go for distributing the proceeds of the sales of the public lands to the several states, to enable our state, in common with others, to dig canals and construct rail roads without borrowing money and paying interest on it." Lincoln's advocacy for internal improvements was not unusual, but his deliberate mention of the sale of public lands signaled his desire for such projects to be accomplished without incurring debt, which the state had recently managed to eliminate for the first time. The question as to how far he would be willing to champion internal improvements without debt would be answered in forthcoming legislative sessions.[33]

"If elected," Lincoln continued, "I shall consider the whole people of Sangamon my constituents, as well those that oppose, as those that support me." This remark might have been political rhetoric. More likely, it was an acknowledgement of the escalating role of party politics in dictating the views and actions of elected officials and that even as a Whig, he intended to reach beyond partisan interests. If that was the case, Lincoln did not attempt to conceal his presidential choice, proudly concluding the letter, "If alive on the first Monday in November, I shall vote for Hugh L. White for President."[34]

Soon after his announcement to the *Journal*, Lincoln faced the first major attack on his character of his political career. In June 1836 Colonel Robert Allen stopped in New Salem. A Democrat and Springfield resident campaigning for the legislature, Allen declared publicly to residents there that he possessed certain facts, which, if generally known, would entirely destroy both Lincoln's and Edwards's chances of re-election. But Allen claimed that out of personal regard for his political opponents, he would not disclose what those facts were. The work of surveying had pulled Lincoln away during Allen's visit, affording him no opportunity for immediate rebuttal. However, upon hearing what Allen said, Lincoln wrote forthrightly to him with assurance that he "had the confidence of the people of Sangamon," and challenged Allen to divulge any alleged facts whether they be "real or supposed." Lincoln even went so far as to imply that his accuser was a "traitor to his country's interest" if he did have confidential information and not release it. While Lincoln's friends referred to Allen as "a bag of wind," Lincoln decided instead to exercise grace and take the moral high ground.[35] He ended his letter to Allen pledging: "Your part, however low it may sink me, shall never break the tie of personal friendship between us."[36] Allen was silenced.

Lincoln's exercise in graciousness did not mean, however, that he always resisted political jabs when given the opportunity. George Forquer had been appointed to the lucrative office of Register of the Land Office, and built a new frame house in Springfield complete with a lightning rod, the first home there with one. When he turned Democrat, Whigs turned against him. At an 1836 campaign speech in Springfield, Forquer pointed to Lincoln, proclaiming that "the young man would have to be taken down." Lincoln considered that a challenge, so he vaulted to the stage to counter. "Mr. Forquer commenced his speech by announcing that the young man would have to be taken down," Lincoln smirked. "It is for you, fellow citizens, not for me to say whether I am up or down. . . . I desire to live, and I desire place and distinction; but I would rather die now than, like the gentleman, live to see the day that I would change my politics for an office worth three thousand dollars a year, and then feel compelled to erect a lightning rod to protect a guilty conscience from an offended God." The crowd erupted in laughter. Forquer's notoriety would be for a long time linked with the lightning rod. For months afterward, whenever Forquer rose to speak, hecklers would say, "There is the man who dare not sleep in his own house without a lightning rod to keep off the vengeance of the Almighty."[37]

Joshua Speed, who months later would become one of Lincoln's most intimate friends, listened to Lincoln's stinging rejoinder to Forquer. Speed recalled, "The speech produced a profound impression, the crowd was with him." Speed heaped praise on the candidate, noting, "I have heard him often since in the courts and before the people, but never saw him appear and acquit himself so well as upon that occasion."[38]

Lincoln's political rise occurred in an era in which people prized political engagement. Though the political culture did not always yield civilized debate, the spirit of democracy prevailed. Men of different classes could freely congregate in equality and mutual respect in meetinghouses, at political rallies, and elsewhere to freely voice their opinions. The French philosopher Alexis de Tocqueville traveled across the ocean in 1831 and 1832 to personally experience the great American democracy at work, publishing his findings in the

1835 book *Democracy in America.* Visiting both farm and city in the northern and southern states, de Tocqueville came away impressed with the extent of civic engagement and participation in the political process in America. He noted that the level of intellectual discourse in the country and the political spirit and regard for personal liberty pervaded the land so intensely that politics had become the civic religion of the nation.[39]

That political energy elicited more contenders than ever for the legislature in the August 1836 election. In all, seventeen candidates entered the state legislative race for the seven Sangamon seats. Seeing that a great number of Jackson supporters were unenthused by Martin Van Buren as successor, Lincoln perceived that his chances of winning over Democrats were favorable among the crowded field of seven Whigs and ten Democrats. But he left little to chance. He actively canvassed for votes by attending party meetings, rallies, and candidate debates to a greater extent than he had in previous campaigns.[40]

In the course of the next few weeks, the candidates stumped all across the county. Often both Whig and Democrat candidates traveled together and appeared jointly. In July in Springfield, Lincoln participated in the first ever Sangamon County state legislative candidates debate, featuring Whigs Lincoln, Edwards, and Dan Stone, and Democrats Jacob Early, John Calhoun, and Richard Quinton.[41] "We traveled on horseback from one grove to another," recalled candidate Robert Wilson. "The speaking would begin in the forenoon, the candidates speaking alternately until all who could speak had his turn, generally consuming the whole afternoon."[42] Voters interrogated the candidates on the future of the state bank, on the extent of internal improvement projects, and on the progress of the Illinois and Michigan Canal construction. One event south of Springfield took Lincoln past Forquer's new home, where he saw the famed lightning rod for the first time.[43]

"Always a Whig" in politics, Lincoln made no apologies for being a politician or a member of the Whigs. "The man who is of neither party," he contended, "is not—cannot be, of any consequence" in society.[44] Lincoln certainly rose to the challenge in the rough and tumble game of party politics, and felt prepared to stick up for his fellow Whig candidates when criticized. The rivalries became so bitter that at an event at the Sangamon County courthouse, candidate Jacob Early challenged Ninian Edwards to a duel. Lincoln then mounted the stage and so subdued the boisterous opposition with his clear shrill voice that "every one was astonished."[45] The *Sangamo Journal* reported that "a girl might be born and become a mother before the Van Buren men will forget Mr. Lincoln."[46] Robert Wilson admitted that in the campaign, Lincoln took "a leading part espousing the Whig side of all those questions, manifesting skill and tact."[47] Even Lincoln felt that now "his reputation was made."[48]

Voters likewise expressed their confidence in him on August 1, 1836. Lincoln won the most votes among seventeen total candidates with a tally of 1,716. The Whig candidates all fared well, and nary a Democrat won a seat.[49] As was the case in 1834, many of Lincoln's Democratic friends voted for him, though he did not receive the organized support he had in that prior run. With hardened political lines, even Jack Armstrong did not vote for Lincoln this time around.[50]

A month later, the Illinois Supreme Court gave Lincoln another step toward becoming an attorney when they granted him a license to practice law in all counties of the state. Shortly thereafter, Lincoln attended Sangamon County Circuit Court as it opened its fall term. However, the opportunity for Lincoln to engross himself in law would have to wait a little longer, for session in Vandalia would begin shortly. He likewise continued in his efforts to promote the Whig presidential candidate Hugh White, who would lose the presidential election in a field of four to Van Buren. Perhaps a small consolation, White took Sangamon County, in no small part due to Lincoln and other Whigs' support. John T. Stuart's loss to William May the following month in the congressional elections proved to be another disappointment for the Whigs.

Lincoln's heartbreak over the death of Ann Rutledge began to lift by 1836. Still a very young man, shortly before departing for Vandalia, he expressed interest in Mary Owens. Lincoln met Kentucky resident Mary Owens three years earlier when she came to visit her sister Elizabeth Abell in New Salem. Abell attempted to play matchmaker, and when she told Lincoln she planned to go to Kentucky to visit

Owens in the autumn of 1836, Lincoln jested that if Abell brought
her sister back to New Salem he might be content to marry her. To
Lincoln's surprise, Abell did so. In their short time together, Owens
and Lincoln developed a fondness for each other and embarked on
a courtship, interrupted by Lincoln's leaving for Vandalia.[51]

On December 5, 1836, Lincoln took his seat for another term in
the Tenth General Assembly. With Stuart no longer in the legislature
things changed for Lincoln, one being his lodging. He now roomed
at the Globe Hotel with Jesse Dubois, Robert Wilson, and Edwin
Webb. Kentucky-born Edwin Webb from White County found
much in common with Lincoln and became a devotee of him in the
legislature.[52] Politically, Stuart's departure paved the way for Lincoln
to fill his shoes. The tutelage under Stuart and his great ability in
the recent campaign to effectively and deftly elevate Whig principles
boosted his support for a leadership position in the legislature. Now
as a second-termer, Lincoln might have an opportunity to be the
Whig floor leader. Jesse Dubois noted, "Lincoln didn't take much
prominence in the first session of the legislature in 1834. But the
next session [in 1836] Lincoln was very prominent. He had by that
time become the acknowledged leader of the Whigs in the House."[53]

The Tenth General Assembly, which met in December 1836, found
sixty-six new legislators, an even larger body of newcomers than in
1834.[54] The reapportionment as a result of the 1835 census contributed
greatly to that, as did voter indignation over the hugely unpopular
"little bull law" from the previous session. In one of its first acts in
the new session, the legislature promptly and wisely repealed that
law. Even before the session began, a feeling of great expectation
greeted the legislature. Newspapers as far removed as Galena in the
northwestern part of the state anticipated this session of members "of
fine talent and sound judgement," giving special mention to "Abraham Lincoln of Sangamon."[55] The *Sangamo Journal* also gave high
praise, touting, "The present legislature embraces, perhaps, more
talent than any legislative body ever before assembled in Illinois."[56]
The ascription might be accurate, as that legislative assembly eventually produced three governors, eight congressman, six U.S. senators,
and one president.[57]

Among the newcomers appeared Democrat Stephen A. Douglas from Morgan County. A lawyer and former teacher, Douglas was spirited and determined and had developed a reputation for political astuteness even before taking his legislative seat. Four years younger than Lincoln, he was a born politician. Merely five feet, four inches tall, Douglas was stout and barrel chested, with thick, dark hair, heavy brows, piercing eyes, and boyish looks. But his true gift lay in his persuasive oratory. He had a vibrant and commanding voice that conveyed depth and passion. When he talked, it was as if his eyes and voice were "shooting out electric fires."[58] Unlike Lincoln, he was gentlemanly and dressed in the finest attire he could afford. But like Lincoln, he could win friends easily and had a genuine desire to rise in the world. He would serve only one legislative term before being appointed to the federal government position of register of the land office in Springfield.

The new friends Lincoln quickly made included freshman representative Archibald Williams. Their proximity at the assembly table gave them the chance to get to know each other. Williams had previously served in the state senate when he lived in Hancock County. Soon after moving to Adams County, he won his House seat in a special election. Lincoln found much to like in Williams. A Kentuckian by birth, the fellow Whig lawyer was over six feet tall. Lincoln described Williams as among the "strongest minded and clearest-headed" men he ever encountered.[59] The pair also shared a disdain for formality. Awkward in gestures, uncouth in manners, untidy in dress, and uncomely in appearance, Williams matched Lincoln fairly. Once, while seated next to each other, a visitor approached them and asked wryly, "Who in the hell are those two ugly men?"[60]

Ireland-born James Shields also arrived for the first time in the Illinois House in 1836. Settling in Randolph County near Kaskaskia in 1826, he took up law. An able lawyer and respected Democratic politician, Shields's unfortunate vanity and hot temper did not win him many friends. His stint in the legislature would be short-lived; in 1839 he would be appointed state auditor.[61]

Another newcomer was the well-educated lawyer from Jacksonville, John J. Hardin. Born in Kentucky, the Morgan County Whig moved to Illinois to practice law and fought in the Black Hawk War. Known to be combative and intellectual, he matched Lincoln in political ambition. A year younger than Lincoln, Hardin's father had been the secretary of state in Kentucky and Hardin aspired to follow in his father's footsteps as a political leader. Although both were Whigs, Lincoln and Hardin never cemented a close personal or political bond.[62]

Usher F. Linder of Coles County also debuted among the 1836 General Assembly. Six feet tall and slender, the well-educated lawyer came from the same Kentucky county as Lincoln. Six weeks younger than Lincoln, Linder arrived in Illinois just one year before winning his election to the legislature. The intelligent lawyer was a powerful and witty speaker ready to challenge anyone to a debate. Even Lincoln soon appreciated the oratorical abilities of the man known as the "terror on the stump."[63] However, he humorously stated that Linder's desire to make speeches owed more to the fact that he liked to hear himself talk. Lincoln said of Linder, "In one faculty, at least, there can be no dispute of the gentleman's superiority over me, and most other men; and that is, the faculty of entangling a subject, so that neither himself, nor any other man, can find head or tail to it."[64] The two would soon find themselves separated by wide political differences.

In the state senate, Orville Browning of Quincy arrived for the first time. The college-educated, Kentucky-born lawyer moved to Adams County in 1831. He and Lincoln became acquainted during the Black Hawk War. The tall, robust man of impressive appearance and marked dignity brought an "old school politeness" to the legislature.[65] His powerful oratory, witnesses said, carried "an eloquence and pathos" that moved juries and audiences to tears.[66] He also brought his wife Eliza, who, upon meeting Lincoln in 1836, immediately adored his genial nature. Lincoln for his part found Mrs. Browning equally charming, and soon felt comfortable enough to confide his private thoughts to her—one of the few women with whom he would ever do so. Many occasions would find Lincoln and the Brownings delighting in shared company. Orville Browning recalled of Lincoln, "He was very fond of Mrs. Browning's society, and spent many of his evenings, and much of his leisure time, at our rooms."[67]

It surely did not take long for observers to detect a unique aspect of the seven representatives and two senators from Sangamon County: they were all nearly six feet tall or taller. Of "the Long Nine," as the group came to be called, William Elkin, a Kentucky-born farmer who fathered fifteen children, was, at forty-five, the oldest. John Dawson, veteran of the War of 1812 and the Black Hawk War, father of ten children, was also forty-five. Dan Stone, a college-educated Vermonter and able lawyer was thirty-six. The adventurous thirty-five-year-old Andrew McCormick, over six feet tall and nearly three hundred pounds, had worked as a stonecutter, lead miner, and Indian fighter, and was the father of ten children. Robert Wilson, age thirty-one, had originated from Pennsylvania and moved westward, occupying himself as a lawyer and teacher. Youngest of the group—he was two months younger than Lincoln—was Ninian Edwards, son of the former governor, whose aristocratic lifestyle in Springfield had made him unpopular. In the Senate, Job Fletcher, age forty-three, father of seven children and War of 1812 veteran, engaged in farming and had been beaten in his three previous attempts for the Illinois House. Archer G. Herndon, forty-one years old and the father of William Herndon, who later became Lincoln's law partner, employed himself as an innkeeper. Dawson held the distinction of the longest serving of the Long Nine, being first elected in 1830. Above all, Lincoln, the colossus of the group, was called "the Sangamon Chief."[68]

With the Long Nine's backing, Lincoln's name surfaced as a candidate for Speaker of the Illinois House of Representatives. The Democrats, however, retained a majority in the House, and accordingly re-elected James Semple to the post. For the coveted position of Whig floor leader, the party stood behind their rising star Abraham Lincoln, and awarded him that position. Democrats, too, recognized Lincoln's leadership abilities and along with the lesser Penitentiary Committee assigned him to the chairmanship of the Finance Committee.[69]

Lincoln's genial, jocular manner and his ability to win friends proved effective for legislative bargaining. He ambled through the chamber, and after hours in the taverns or in his lodging, working the men of the legislature. With a quick joke, a back slap, or a handshake, he could then and there effectively consummate a deal.[70] Joseph Gillespie, whom Lincoln served with in the legislature, observed that "Mr. Lincoln had the appearance of being a slow thinker. My impression is that he was not [so much] slow as he was careful. . . . His qualities were those ordinarily given to mankind but he had them in a remarkable degree. . . . He had an immense stock of common sense." On his personable nature, Gillespie noted, "He was genial but not very sociable. . . . But when he was in [the company of others], he was the most entertaining person I ever knew."[71]

Though entertaining, all was not well with Lincoln. The cold December weather, the clamminess of the Vandalia statehouse, and the melancholy wore upon him physically and emotionally. He had developed feelings for Mary Owens, and now apart from her he realized he had grown fond of her and missed her. He expected that she might write to him, but she had not done so. His affection seemingly unrequited, a week into session, Lincoln wrote to Owens, "I have been sick ever since my arrival here." Admitting his lowly emotional state, he relayed, "I believe I am about well now; but that, with other things I cannot account for, have conspired and have gotten my spirits so low, that I feel that I would rather be any place in the world than here. I really cannot endure the thought of staying here ten weeks."[72] Lincoln's rise politically was little match for the melancholy that would grip him occasionally throughout his life.

In his letter to Owens, Lincoln expressed displeasure at the course of action thus far in the legislature. "The new State House is not yet finished, and consequently the legislature is doing little or nothing," he lamented. Indeed, when the General Assembly arrived for their session in December 1836, they found a new capitol building under construction yet very far from completion.[73]

A question on the November 1834 ballot statewide had asked voters of their preference if the state capital were to move. In the results, Alton edged out Vandalia, and Springfield came in third. The people of New Salem cast 250 votes, out of 256 possible, for Springfield.[74] Though the vote was nonbinding, it did draw considerable interest. Sensing that the stage was set for relocation, in 1836 the citizens of Vandalia decided to preempt a move, and, at their own expense, raised the funds to build a new statehouse. The city hoped that the legislature would recognize their efforts, reimburse them, and retain the capital in Vandalia. The new House and Senate chambers occupied opposing wings of the second floor, complete with a balcony for visitors. The requisite tables, chairs, and spittoons lined the room. But by December, the building stood unfinished—the yard still covered with piles of bricks, lumber, and waste. The plaster in the interior of the House chamber had not yet dried, emitting a cold and musty dampness.[75]

Governor Joseph Duncan addressed the legislature regarding the new building, extending appreciation to Vandalia citizens. He stated, "In consequence of the dilapidated and falling condition of the old State House . . . the citizens of this place, believing that the legislature would have no place to convene or hold their session, have built the House you now occupy." With a nod to the efforts of the citizens to retain the capital in Vandalia, he acknowledged that the city of Vandalia "commands our grateful acknowledgements, and I hope their services and expenses will be promptly remunerated."[76]

Even with the attempt of Vandalians to thwart relocation, Lincoln sensed the changing winds and the ripening opportunity to lead the charge for a move. He relayed in his letter to Mary Owens that the prospects for capital relocation were "better than I expected."[77] The prospects were positive, not only because of the shift northward of the population, but because the results of the Illinois census of 1835 compelled the legislature to reapportion state representation. Areas with increased population, especially Sangamon County, would have more legislative clout in an anticipated push for capital relocation northward.

Governor Duncan used his legislative address to berate the policies of President Jackson, who had only three months left in his presidency. Such statements were certain to create a firestorm in the Democratic state of Illinois. Kentucky native Duncan had moved to Jacksonville, Illinois, the year it became a state in 1818, and not long afterward gained election to Congress. A Democrat early on, Duncan found himself aligning more with the Whigs in voting against President Jackson's policies. The final straw came in 1834 when Duncan voted for the recharter of the Bank of the United States. Deciding to return to Illinois in 1834, he allowed the Democrats to campaign for him for governor, without informing them that he no longer belonged to their party. Winning that year, he became the only Whig governor in Illinois history. Now in 1836 a climate of partisanship hung over the legislature, a holdover from the presidential election a month earlier.[78] Duncan's denunciation of Jackson led Lincoln to expect there to be some "sparring between the parties" as soon as the General Assembly set to business.[79] Lincoln predicted correctly the Democratic response. Representative John McClernand of Gallatin, a rising Democratic Party leader, submitted a stern rebuke to Duncan, to which the Whigs promptly submitted an equally firm defense of the governor.[80]

Beyond the partisan diatribe, the governor recommended that the legislature fund public education. The majority of his address, however, detailed his encouragement that the legislature craft a wholesale internal improvements bill to include road, bridge, harbor, canal, and railroad improvements.[81] Duncan happily declared that "Illinois is fast ascending in the scale of importance and will in a short time take her station among the first states of the Union." He nudged the legislature, saying that the grandeur of Illinois would "in a great degree, depend on her future legislation."[82] He dreamt of a state "intersected by canals and railroads, and our beautiful prairies enlivened by thousands of steam engines."[83] However, as in the previous session, Duncan worried about the state's assuming too much debt. He cautioned against the legislature's selling state bonds to pursue internal improvements projects. Promises on paper, he argued, were not dependable enough for a reliable stream of capital. Instead, just as he had recommended to the legislature a year earlier, he advised that the state should assume no more than half the financial obligation necessary for internal improvements.[84]

The push for internal improvements beginning in 1834 now reached fever pitch. "No state in the Union," stated an observer, "possesses such facilities for intercommunication by canals and railways, at so cheap rate as Illinois."[85] A mass public meeting in Springfield held before the session gave unequivocal support for a general system of internal improvements, and citizens there tagged their legislators from Sangamon County with the demand, "It is now time TO ACT" (emphasis theirs).[86] "It is not a party measure," the *Sangamo Journal* recorded of the meeting's declarations, "and all our citizens can cordially unite in one vigorous effort to secure the adoption of a system of Internal Improvements for this State, which is so much desired, and so absolutely necessary to its prosperity."[87] A similar state convention in Vandalia comprised of delegates from the many counties held shortly after the session's opening recommended construction of wide-scale projects, particularly railroads in accordance "with the wants of the people."[88] Delegates at the Vandalia convention resolved that the system should be financed by whatever means necessary, except through taxation.[89]

While Whigs had long embraced internal improvements, advocacy within the state for such projects knew no party distinction. In mid-December 1836, Stephen Douglas got the ball rolling by introducing a series of internal improvement proposals to the floor of the House that included plans for the construction of north-south and east-west railroad lines, canal building, road, river, and turnpike constructions, and "surveys and estimates of other such works as may be considered of general utility."[90] Douglas's proposal asked for the state's credit to construct the projects. Lincoln applauded Douglas's measure while internal improvements enjoyed bipartisan support.[91] If the legislature did little or nothing early on, they now sprang into action. Legislators rushed to propose what projects, how many, and where they might be. Every county wanted a railroad to pass through it, or a canal over its river, or an improved waterway or road to travel within it. Every legislator considered the applause he would receive by bringing home such improvements to his region. Sangamon County representatives likewise weighed the possible projects within their reach.[92] Beginning on December 19 and for several days following, the House acted as a committee on internal improvements and discussed a litany of additions to Douglas's bill.[93]

Illinois legislators imagined the possibilities and made their proposals. A railroad could connect Cairo in the far southern reaches of the state to Galena and its lead mines in the far northwestern corner. Quincy in the western edge of the state could connect through Springfield to Danville in the east. Peoria in the central part of the state could connect with Shelbyville and down to Terre Haute, Indiana. Bloomington in the state's middle might connect with Peoria. Edwardsville near St. Louis might extend to Shawneetown just west of the Kentucky border. Alton, near St. Louis, would be the terminus of several rail lines. The plan did not include a railroad connecting Chicago since it would have the Illinois and Michigan Canal linking it to other parts of the state.[94] In all, the plan included more than thirteen hundred miles of rail.[95] With the fury of railroad proposals, there seemed to be little planning for the regulation and oversight of construction.[96] Legislators also failed to calculate cost. They reasoned that just as with the Erie Canal in New York, usage fees from the Illinois and Michigan Canal would result in revenue in the state coffers of Illinois. A few legislators disagreed, proposing a property tax to pay for the projects; however, such voices of dissent remained in the minority. [97]

For the governance and operation of internal improvement projects, the legislature created two different boards. Three fund commissioners would raise money. They were also to direct profits from the Bank of Illinois to pay for the Illinois and Michigan Canal and other projects. Therefore, the fate of the state bank and that of the canal—now estimated to be a $13 million project—were interwoven.[98] Then there would be a public works board of seven who would manage the contracts and construction of the railroads and rivers. Both boards would be selected by and answerable to the state legislature.[99]

The Long Nine had two goals for the 1836–37 session: to pass the internal improvements bill; and to relocate the state capital from Vandalia to Springfield. Broad public support for civic improvements across the state created the temptation for logrolling. The Long Nine figured they could support the many projects of other legislators in return for a promise of support for something that they and their Sangamon County constituents coveted: relocation of the state capital to Springfield.[100] So they went to work. Some historians have contended the Long Nine did not engage in a vote swap of internal improvements in exchange for capital relocation. However, considering the clout the Long Nine wielded, it is politically naïve to suspect there was no pressure put on fellow legislators to vote for both.[101]

The trading of votes, or logrolling, had long been a tool for getting legislation passed at all levels of politics. Representative John Hardin shook his head at how "members support measures they would not otherwise vote for, to obtain another member's vote." Calling the state legislature a "den of legislative trading," he wrote that no one is truly at home there unless he is willing to "debase himself to bargain and trade."[102] The Long Nine saw that traditional political tool as a means to achieve their aims, and exercised it. They believed in the cause of internal improvements, but even more wished for the relocation of the capital, and were all too happy to exchange support for improvement projects for capital-removal support. Ensuring the removal became, in Stephen Douglas's words, "the all-absorbing topic" for the Sangamon delegation.[103] The Long Nine were not always united on every vote, but when they were, not only did the Sangamon County legislators possess influence on the floor, but as the largest delegation in the state, they held immense legislative power publicly and behind the scenes.[104] "The gigantic and stupendous operations of the [Long Nine] scheme dazzled the eyes of nearly everybody," wrote William Herndon.[105]

That maneuvering did raise the indignation of some. Morgan County representative Richard Walker protested the market of "bargain and sale that was brought about to make Springfield the successful candidate."[106] Representative Christian Blockburger witnessed "how votes were swapped off and exchanged, and how quickly the local measures of other members were voted for, when Springfield could receive a vote in return."[107] Thomas Ford, a judge in western Illinois who later became governor attended some of the 1836–37 session and observed the proceedings. When it came to logrolling, Ford noted, the Long Nine "rolled like a snowball."[108] No move of support or opposition on the part of the Long Nine made during that term "was . . . [ever] without a bargain for votes in return on the seat of government question." Calling the Long Nine Whigs "demagogues," he contended that "they gathered strength for the Springfield move-ment that way by giving internal improvement projects in return for a vote for the move."[109] The political horse-trading led Ford to conclude: "By giving the seat of government to Springfield, was the whole state bought up and bribed."[110]

Members of the Long Nine themselves admitted their sway. Rob-ert Wilson later stated, "We were not only noted for our number and length, but for our combined influence." "All the bad or objection-able laws passed at that session of the Legislature and for many years afterwards," Wilson continued, "were chargeable to the management and influence of the 'Long Nine.'" Not denying the political tactics they employed, Wilson said flatly, "Many and ingenious were the maneuvers, but it would fill page after page to narrate them."[111] He regretted his part in the scheme, and later as a member of Congress lamented the logrolling that happened in Illinois.[112]

It is not known what role Lincoln had in behind-the-scenes ma-neuvering, though as the "chief" likely no such actions were without his knowledge or approval. Stephen T. Logan claimed Lincoln to be the head of the relocation efforts. "It was entirely entrusted to him to manage. The members . . . all looked to Lincoln as their head."[113] Wilson contended that Lincoln "was on the stump and in the halls of the Legislature a ready debater, manifesting extraordinary ability in his peculiar manner of presenting his subject."[114] Lincoln himself freely admitted that he went beyond mere persuasion, disclosing to Jesse Dubois that he "had traded off everything he could dispose of." Lincoln confided, "I can't go home without passing that bill. My folks expect that of me." Lincoln declared that if the mission failed, "I am finished forever."[115] He learned to wield political tools to achieve larger political aims, a strategy he would similarly employ as president in passing the Thirteenth Amendment that abolished slavery.

Dubois defended Lincoln's actions as part of the political process and insisted he participated in no wrongdoing nor did anything underhanded. "Lincoln was always a good man," said Dubois. "He never played tricks on anybody."[116] For his own part Lincoln defended his motives. In a passionate late-night speech on the House floor, he pronounced, "You may burn my body to the ashes, and scatter them to the winds of heaven . . . but you will never get me to support a measure which I believe to be wrong, although by doing so I may accomplish that which I believe to be right."[117] Joshua Speed agreed that once Lincoln decided a course of action to be the correct one he would seldom deviate from that position. He said of Lincoln, "Unlike all other men there was entire harmony between his public and private life. He must believe that he was right and that he had truth and justice with him or he was a weak man. But no man could be stronger if he thought that he was right."[118]

To ensure the needed internal improvements victory in the House, Lincoln convened the Long Nine and other like-minded representatives together in his room. Robert Wilson of the Long Nine reflected on these episodes, "When our bill, to all appearance was dead . . . and our friends could see no hope, Lincoln never for a moment despaired, but collected his colleagues in his room for consultation."[119] He assigned them each to call upon representatives who were on the fence and persuade them to support the bill. Some representatives were to be reminded that they owed the Sangamon County delegation gratitude for including their respective projects in the internal improvements bill.[120]

Not content to remain on the sidelines, several Springfield citizens joined in the efforts, traveling to Vandalia to push the Long Nine and to lobby other legislators. Peter Van Bergen recorded that "Stuart, Logan, Iles, & I went down to Vandalia. . . . I helped a great deal to drum up the members when it came to a vote. . . . I used to go to them to the saloons &c. I spent about $1000 in treating & c."[121] Stephen Logan, however, refuted the notion that he personally went to Vandalia to pressure legislative members to vote for the bill. In fact, Logan stated he stood in opposition to it. He recounted, "I was in Vandalia that winter and had a talk with Lincoln there. I took him to task for voting for the Internal Improvement scheme. He seemed to acquiesce in the correctness of my views as I presented them to him. But he said he couldn't help himself—he had to vote for it in order to secure the removal here of the seat of government."[122]

Even if vote trading figured in Lincoln's ardent backing of internal improvements, as a devotee of the Whig school of Henry Clay he subscribed to the theory that internal improvements would grow the whole economy of Illinois. In his estimation, there could be nothing wrong with building a canal here, or deepening a river there, or expanding the railroad here and there—all of which were certain to be factors for economic growth. For instance, he spoke in support of a $50,000 appropriation for improvement of Big Muddy Creek, a state road from Springfield to Bloomington, and $320,000 to build a railroad from Bloomington to Pekin. Lincoln championed such projects, even telling a friend that he wanted to be known as the "DeWitt Clinton of Illinois," after the famed New York governor who helped birth the Erie Canal.[123]

The internal improvements bill nearly hit a snag when some legislators, concerned with the breadth of the bill, proposed that the package be submitted directly to the people for their vote. But the majority, Lincoln included, believed it was their due authority to decide whether or not to appropriate money to projects, and the amendment failed.[124]

Attempts were also made to merge the funding of schools with the internal improvements plan, and legislators proposed that $25,000 in loans be made to each county for schools. While Lincoln always advocated education as a worthy goal, he believed that school funding necessitated its own separate bill and voted against such inclusions in the internal improvements bill. As a more equitable means of distribution, legislators several times proposed that school funding be allocated not at a uniform rate, but rather per the number of children under twenty years of age who lived in each county. Lincoln voted no on that proposal, and offered his own amendment that the money be distributed according to county lines that existed before the 1835 census, which also met defeat.[125] An overall school-funding bill did pass, with Lincoln giving it his enthusiastic support. In supporting funding for public schools, Illinois took its first serious step toward recognizing the government's role in education.[126]

The population surge in central and northern Illinois spurred renewed interest in Sangamon County division. But the arrival in Vandalia of a land speculator caused an unexpected maelstrom. Democrat John Taylor journeyed to the state capital from Sangamon County armed with a petition that demanded a new county be created out of the northern section of Sangamon County and part of Morgan County. Taylor had an ulterior motive: to divide Sangamon and move the state capital to Illiopolis where he owned land.[127] Seeking an opportunity to weaken Sangamon County, Usher Linder from Coles County then hopped on to the county-division effort, proposing that the northwestern part of Sangamon County—from where Lincoln hailed—be split off and named for Martin Van Buren.[128]

Lincoln took tremendous interest in Sangamon County's division, having been elected partly on the basis of that platform. But Taylor's petition left Lincoln and the Long Nine in a quandary. Lincoln worried that division of the state's largest county would leave it with a decreased number of representatives, which would dilute their legislative influence and damage the capital relocation effort. Yet he did not wish to go on record as being against the division. Weighing his options, Lincoln took to the newspaper. The *Sangamo Journal* ran a piece written under the name Rusticus that was likely authored by Lincoln. The article criticized those who wished to divide Sangamon into "pea-patch counties," charging that "dangerous speculators" and selfish office-seekers were leading such efforts.[129]

To buy time, Lincoln then astutely moved that the petition be taken out of the hands of the full House, and be referred to a select committee comprised of three representatives, including Robert Wilson and himself. For tactical reasons, Lincoln's committee's report ensured that the petition included in the proposed new county part of Morgan County, in the hope that it might trigger opposition from representatives of that county. The tactic succeeded in drawing the ire of both John Hardin and Stephen Douglas from Morgan. Douglas's Committee on Petitions also took up the issue, and within days released their report. They recommended the division of Sangamon County and the removal of Morgan County from consideration in the bill. Hoping to further derail the bill and buy more time, Lincoln proposed an amendment that final acceptance should be up to the voters of Sangamon County, and not the legislature. A petition would be circulated in Sangamon County and all other counties affected by divisions to make an accounting of names of all who approved and disapproved. Douglas agreed, perhaps viewing it as a popular sovereignty issue.[130]

To gain favor among constituents back home, Lincoln requested that three thousand copies of his own committee's recommendation report be printed at state expense and distributed to Sangamon County residents for their review. Usher Linder protested, voicing disapproval over the needless expense for what he viewed as a pro-paganda campaign. Lincoln responded that it seemed uncourteous "for the gentleman from Coles to meddle in the matter at all." Linder thundered that if Lincoln and the Sangamon group wanted the report printed they could do so out of their own pockets. "They are rich enough, God knows: they hold the bag, like Judas," he proclaimed. "I have but little love for Sangamo. It has as little claim upon the generosity of the democracy of this state, as any portion of God's heritage." Linder then continued the assault, praying that Lincoln's farce would defeat him in the next election, saying, "Mr. Speaker, I would advise the gentleman to move for the printing of 3,000 copies of this report for the especial benefit of his constituents. But before you do, consider awhile whether your constituents may not teach you another courtesy." Lincoln mocked in reply, "What marvelous talents some gentlemen possessed, and how determined they are that the House and the world should have the benefit of them." The motion to print the report failed, so Lincoln ensured that it instead appeared in the *Sangamo Journal*.[131]

Sangamon County took up the directive for county division petitions. In February 1836, the results reached Vandalia. There were 2,213 names in opposition and 1,437 in favor.[132] But charges of corruption soon flew alleging that John Taylor had obtained signatures by paying people to sign the petition, and that signatures from road petitions were clipped and added to the division petition. Additionally, more than one hundred people signed twice. Archer Herndon described the petition as "barefaced corruption," and Ninian Edwards charged that "villainous proceedings have taken place to deceive the people."[133]

Laying the petition results aside, the House decided to take up the Sangamon County division on its own. The Long Nine wanted county division more favorable to the likings of their county, so Archer Herndon of Sangamon took care that the attempt perished in the Senate. Thus, for now the division of Sangamon would again be postponed. Before the county division debate died in this session, Douglas proposed the formation of a new county from Stark and Peoria, which Lincoln supported. The bill passed, but the county never organized. It would have been named Coffee County.[134]

Proposed internal improvements, 1837. This map shows the mass of projects proposed as part of the 1837 internal improvements system, most of which never materialized. From William Nida, *The Story of Illinois and Its People* (Chicago: O. P. Barnes, 1910).

WINNING LEGISLATION,
WINNING ESTEEM

Midway through the 1836–37 session Lincoln excused himself from proceedings to return to New Salem. It is not known why he left; perhaps he longed to see Mary Owens. Absent for a week, he returned to plunge into the most consequential and controversial issues facing the state: the state bank, internal improvements, and capital relocation.

The reprise of the bank issue did not surprise Lincoln. The legislature approved the new Bank of Illinois charter two years earlier, but bank opponents charged mismanagement, similar to what sunk the original state bank. To lead the opposition Democrats selected the formidable Usher Linder. He introduced a series of resolutions calling for a committee of seven to investigate the Bank of Illinois in Springfield and in Shawneetown, alleging that the inept bank commissioners had been bribed in distributing loans. Now, bank supporters needed an equal spokesman to squelch the opposition, and for that task Lincoln stood primed and ready.

Lincoln immediately sent allies to Springfield on a fact-finding mission regarding the bank's condition and practices. Friends there equipped him with counterarguments. With those tucked under his arm, in a lengthy speech on the House floor Lincoln inveighed against Linder. He refuted the need for an investigation, and censured Linder for making an issue where there was none, remarking, "No one can doubt that the examination proposed by this resolution, must cost the State some ten or twelve thousand dollars; and all this to settle a question in which the people have no interest, and about which they care nothing." Lincoln then questioned that if bank commissioners could be bribed, then a legislative committee selected by Linder to examine the bank could be likewise bribed. That charge infuriated Linder, and he called Lincoln out of order, then reconsidered and withdrew his appeal, stating he would allow Lincoln to "break his own neck." Lincoln derisively thanked Linder for his "gracious condescension." Denying himself as a "special advocate" for the bank, Lincoln argued that the state legislature had no special authority over the bank, nor did it have the constitutional right to take special powers of investigation. Characterizing such examinations as "lawless and mobocratic," Lincoln declared in satisfaction, "To those who claim omnipotence for the Legislature, and who in the plenitude of their assumed powers, are disposed to disregard the Constitution, law, good faith, moral right, and everything else, I have not a word to say."[1]

The *Sangamo Journal* evaluated Lincoln's leadership, writing that "our friend carries the true Kentucky rifle, and when he fires he seldom fails of sending the shot home."[2] But Lincoln's eloquence failed to persuade Linder, who moved ahead with the idea of a House committee of investigation. Pleased that his speech may have effectively brought a consensus of the House to his side, Lincoln called for a vote on Linder's resolution. As he guessed, Linder's resolution met defeat. However, the Senate took up similar investigation resolutions, and despite Lincoln's opposition, the resolution mustered its way through the House as well. In the end, only a limited examination of the banks occurred, and examiners found nothing unusual or suspicious.[3]

While the state bank debate raged in the halls of the legislature, so did the internal improvements bill. However far the state legislature desired to walk in step with Governor Duncan in support of internal improvements, the majority of the legislature declined to follow the governor's advice that the state shoulder no more than a third of the burden of associated costs. The legislature had hoped investors from the East would realize the potential benefit that improvements such as railroad networks in Illinois might yield and lend crucial financing. That money, however, largely failed to materialize.[4] Where investors did provide funding, legislators grew concerned that private investment would evolve into monopolies over public projects. The assembly also hoped to get the extensive projects under way as soon as possible so as to compete with the other economically flourishing eastern states.[5] So rather than wait for private investment, the legislature decided the projects should, in Lincoln's words, be advanced "on the faith of the State."[6]

No matter how worthy the projects, they would severely test the state's finances—something of which Lincoln, as chairman of the Finance Committee, should have been acutely aware. The state received revenue primarily from taxes on nonresident landowners as well as from income from the state bank loans. Lincoln's Finance Committee report found that after expenses the state balance stood at just over $2,000.[7] When the internal improvements bill came out of the Internal Improvements Committee, it called for $7 million for a statewide north-south railroad with additional smaller east-west lines, $100,000 for all road improvements, and $400,000 for dredging of rivers.[8] Such eye-popping numbers did not seem to bother Lincoln, who, according to William Herndon, had little "money sense."[9] But Lincoln was not alone; the numbers seemed not to disturb the majority of the state legislators who eagerly supported the projects.

Following intense back and forth debate, the legislature recommitted the improvements bill back to committee where Lincoln defended it forcefully. When the bill came before the House again, not only had it not been scaled back, it had expanded! The railroad part of the bill now called for a construction of spurs into several towns along the rail route, as well as $200,000 in cash grants for the state's sixteen counties who had no projects in the bill. No doubt, the bill's crafting came as a result of the Long Nine and of Lincoln's political promises and persuasion. All told, the internal improvements bill's sum reached a hefty $10 million—in a state that had only roughly $5 million in total state tax revenue.[10]

Some in the legislature argued for the necessity of cutting back the massive bill, cautioning that it would plunge the state into debt and lead to bankruptcy. A few lone Whigs, such as freshman representative John J. Hardin of Morgan County, attempted to restrict the bill. He harped that the state would suffer "severely for its unfortunate results."[11] Some outside the legislature voiced concern as well. But a louder contingency of supporters that included Lincoln appealed to "the patriot and enlightened statesman of Illinois" to approve the wholesale system.[12] He and others argued that the large projects, similar to the Erie Canal, would pay for themselves as profits from commercial trade came in. They also still claimed that ready investors and speculators would compete for the sale of state bonds, and the bidding war would drive up the figure so high that the premiums on the bonds would pay for themselves.[13] Bonds in Illinois, proponents promised, would "go like hot cakes."[14] With no assured way for the state to pay for the extravagant internal improvements, the upbeat spirit of the state legislature prevailed.

In late January 1837, the House passed the internal improvements bill, and it equally sailed through the Senate. Governor Duncan flatly vetoed the measure, apprehensive about excessive spending. However, in February, an override of the veto moved through both houses of the General Assembly, easily passing the House 53 to 20.[15] Upon announcing news of its passage, Vandalia illuminated with bonfires and torches. Of the passage of the bill, the *Illinois State Register* declared: "We have no doubt the passage of the bill has already increased the value of the land in the State more than 100 percent; and every day is adding to its value."[16]

Increase the value it did. Speculators rushed in to cash in on the availability of land. Even industrious pioneers crowded into land offices to acquire the valuable property. At that moment, passage of the long-awaited internal improvements bill seemed like the best thing Illinois had ever done. Contemplating the impact of the bill on the state's future, the *Register* continued, "We have the utmost confidence that every acre of the public land will, in a few years, be settled by immigrants, who will add to the population of the State, will increase its wealth, its influence and power among the other states of the confederacy. If the present legislature had done no more, they would have deserved the thanks of the People for the passage of this law."[17]

"On the subject of internal improvements the young giant of the West is making herculean efforts," noted an observer in 1837. "When the public works, which are now advancing with all possible speed, are completed and in successful operation, Illinois will vie with any state in our republic."[18] For now, the legislature looked heroic.

Even before the internal improvements bill had passed, intense deliberation swirled around the relocation of the state capital. Though the citizens of Vandalia constructed their new statehouse without authorization of the state legislature, the majority of the legislature felt compelled to assist the people of Vandalia who fronted the money to build the new statehouse. Lincoln recognized the good will of Vandalia, and voted with the majority. The legislature granted $10,378 toward the construction.[19]

But such funding did not necessarily indicate satisfaction with Vandalia as the permanent capitol. An 1819 law dictating Vandalia as the "permanent" capitol had a twenty-year clause in it, meaning it would expire in two years in 1839. Lincoln moved to repeal the law to set in motion the capital relocation process. That met fierce opposition from Fayette County representative John Dement who lived near Vandalia. Meanwhile in the Senate, Orville Browning officially introduced a capital relocation bill. When the bill came to the House, Alexander Dunbar of Coles County offered several amendments, authored behind the scenes primarily by Lincoln and heavily backed by the Long Nine. The amendments stipulated that any relocation would be contingent upon the ability of citizens of the new city to donate "fifty thousand dollars . . . not less than two acres upon which to erect public buildings . . . without expense to the State." The move was clever since the Sangamon delegation knew that Springfield would be more likely able to meet this condition than other cities. Lincoln had also learned a thing or two about parliamentary procedure. Lincoln sent the Dunbar amendments through the Senate first, with the hope that if the Senate passed the measure, it would see less opposition in the House.[20] Opponents of relocation attempted to table the bill until the next session but that obstructionist move failed by a handful of votes.[21]

In late February 1837, just days before the session expired, the House and Senate met in a joint session to finally vote on the location for the permanent seat of government. The fact that Springfield was more geographically centered in the state bode well for its prospects.

In the first round of balloting, Springfield led with 35 votes, Vandalia came in the next closest with 16 votes, and many other votes were scattered among other cities as legislators cast support for their home communities. Springfield's lead increased with each successive balloting, and clearly the momentum swung in that city's favor. Finally by the fourth and final ballot, Springfield tallied 73 votes, followed by Vandalia with 16 votes, Jacksonville with 11, then Peoria, Alton, and Illiopolis receiving just less than 10. Six other towns received one vote each, including a vote for the Lawrence County town of Purgatory.[22]

There were southern Illinois representatives who ended up voting for relocation of the capital to Springfield. Jesse Dubois counted himself among them. "We belonged to the southern end of the State," Dubois later recalled. "We defended our vote before our constituents by saying that necessity would ultimately force the seat of government to a central position." The Whig legislator acknowledged Lincoln's vital role concluding, "In reality we gave the vote to Lincoln because we liked him and because we wanted to oblige our friend, and because we recognized his authority as our leader."[23] Likewise Henry Webb from White County in southern Illinois wanted the capital to remain in Vandalia but instead deferred to Lincoln out of admiration and "the inability to resist his importunities."[24]

Lincoln made a final motion to amend the bill to read that "the General Assembly reserves the right to repeal this act at any time hereafter."[25] Lincoln's amendment, however, served merely as window dressing since any future relocation would be extremely difficult. The die was cast. The General Assembly passed the relocation bill on February 28, 1837.[26] The capital would move to Springfield. Not all were pleased. Future governor Thomas Ford groused that relocation would cost the state about $6 million, and even half of that amount "would have purchased all the real estate in that town" three times over.[27]

Afterward at the nearby tavern of Ebeneezer Capps the victors celebrated, inviting the entire legislature. The party atmosphere, free champagne, cigars, and oysters tantalized the taste buds enough that many of the legislature's relocation opponents showed up, as well as some stragglers not part of the assembly.[28] Ninian Edwards graciously picked up the tab, which totaled over $223.[29]

When word of the vote reached Springfield, the town lit up with excitement the likes of which had never been seen there before. Citizens rejoiced, building a huge bonfire in the public square. Almost immediately prominent citizens pledged the required $50,000, Lincoln among them. Townsfolk saluted the men who had diligently worked to secure the relocation, above all Abraham Lincoln.[30]

Beyond these more memorable measures, the House and Senate in the 1836–37 session again took up their constitutional duty of electing a United States senator. The Long Nine united behind Whig colleague Archibald Williams of Quincy. With the party balance tilted toward the Democrats however, he lost to a circuit judge and former state representative Richard Young. Unfortunately, Young did not have an impressive start. He and his supporters, including Stephen Douglas, celebrated their victory at a Vandalia saloon. The party grew larger, louder, and eventually got out of control, leaving Young to pay $600 for damages.[31]

That session witnessed more partisan division. Democrats took up a measure to honor the anniversary of Jackson's 1815 victory at the Battle of New Orleans, which was naturally followed by the Whigs crying foul. Hardin protested that with subjects as vitally important as internal improvements, the state bank, and education, it would be inexpedient and improper to consume the legislature's time "acting upon any resolutions which merely involve national politics."[32] That plea fell on deaf ears, as the resolution passed.

Other actions in this session included several petitions requesting permission to "persons who are desirous of being divorced," a matter that, a few years later, would be turned over to county courts.[33] Voters took little notice of an act granting state legislators a one-third per diem increase in salary.[34] And the legislature may not have realized then the significance of an act passed near the session's end in March 1837, granting an official city incorporation charter for the fast-rising burg of Chicago.[35]

On one of the final days of the session, state representative Lincoln offered his first endorsement of antislavery principles. Governor Duncan had earlier brought attention to memorials passed by Southern state legislatures condemning abolitionist societies. Those Southern states

invited Northern states to pass in tandem similar antiabolition memorials. Abolitionist societies had been around since the nation's founding,
but such groups were largely religiously affiliated and in Illinois in
1837 antislavery sentiment found little mainstream support. In fact,
just a little over a decade earlier, the state legislature nearly succeeded
in passing a bill that would have overturned the state's constitutional
prohibition on slavery. The public generally believed that abolitionists,
residing primarily in the North, were encouraging slaves in the South
to rebel. If Northern state legislatures denounced abolitionist societies,
it would send a stern warning to dangerous abolitionists.[36]

As a result, in January 1837 the legislature approved resolutions
denouncing abolitionists as "fire brands of discord and disunion."[37]
The measures disowned any recognition of abolition societies, and
affirmed the sacred constitutional right of Southern states to permit
slavery. Additionally, the resolutions disapproved of any attempt by
Congress to abolish slavery in the District of Columbia without the
consent of the people in that district. Lincoln's limited role in the
bill itself was an amendment stating that Congress had no right
to interfere with slavery in the District of Columbia, "unless the
people of said district petition for the same."[38] The amendment met
defeat. Overall, Lincoln viewed abolitionists as most Illinois politicians did—as dangerous and angry fanatics bent on subverting law
and property rights, who were willing to injure lives to end slavery.
He rejected the use of radicalism and violence as means to an end.
However, his conscience still led him to disagree with the spirit of
the resolutions, as did only five others in the entire Illinois General
Assembly who voted against the January resolutions. Joining him
in the small opposition were Gideon Minor of Edgar County, John
Murphy of Vermilion, Parvin Paullen of Pike, and fellow Sangamon
representatives Andrew McCormick and Dan Stone.[39]

On March 3, 1837, after a very active session, with the primary
legislative business on internal improvements, the state bank, and
state capital relocation approved, the House readied to adjourn and
several members had already left town. But Lincoln and Dan Stone
lingered to enter a protest into the *House Journal.* The two desired
before adjournment to further explain their dissenting votes on the

abolitionist resolutions from six weeks earlier. In the protest, Lincoln and Stone agreed with the legislative majority regarding the danger of abolitionism, stating "that the promulgation of abolition doctrines tends rather to increase than to abate its evils." However, they equally railed against the institution of slavery, declaring it "founded on both injustice and bad policy." They further asserted that Congress had no power to abolish slavery in the states except for in the District of Columbia, where even there it could happen only at the request of the residents of the District.[40]

Lincoln and Stone carefully sidestepped any sympathy with the cause of abolitionists. Neither did their protest carry any strong, moralistic, antislavery language so associated with Lincoln later in life. However, nothing obliged the pair to enter their protest. It did not come as a result of, or on the heels of, any intense debate over slavery. Nothing compelled them other than conscience and principle. They stood to gain nothing politically by declaring in writing that slavery was unjust and wrongful, and it opened them up to possible criticism. In fact, of the six who voted against the January House resolutions, Lincoln found only Dan Stone willing to join him in the March protest. In a state that cared little about the injustice of slavery, and none at all for the welfare of the black race, Lincoln and Stone's protest could rightly be considered courageous. The act demonstrated Lincoln's readiness to define his antislavery position, a stance that would remain forever core to his belief system. That Lincoln later included his protest word for word in his 1860 autobiography—and did not give one mention to any other act from his entire legislative service—indicates that he proudly considered this protest his crowning achievement as an Illinois state representative.[41]

* * *

Just days before departing for home that March of 1837, the Illinois Supreme Court entered Lincoln's name on the list of attorneys registered with the state. The last requirement for practicing law satisfied, he earned the status of full-fledged attorney. With little in his future to be hopeful about a few years prior, he now claimed the titles of State Representative Abraham Lincoln and

Abraham Lincoln, Esquire. Lincoln had advanced greatly in a short amount of time, participating integrally in one of the most signifi-cant legislative sessions in Illinois history. Showcasing his abilities of character, courage, and coercion, he could rightly assert that as a representative of his constituents, he advocated for them well.

That is not to say that Lincoln had escaped the seedy side of politics. In the course of the bank debate, he pejoratively described politicians (including himself) as "a set of men who have interests aside from the interests of the people, and who . . . are, taken as a mass, at least one long step removed from honest men."[42]Lincoln candidly admitted the difficulty of playing the political game while preserving one's integrity and maintaining the respect of others.[43]

With the session behind him, Lincoln pocketed the $100 he had received in December and the $312 from March, including the ad-ditional $4 addendum for each twenty miles of travel, and left Van-dalia.[44] For all his legislative success, he was leaving with a heavy heart. William Butler accompanied Lincoln on horseback to New Salem, and saw unease in his face. Probing his apprehension, Lincoln confided in him, "I am going home, Butler, without a thing in the world. I have drawn all my pay I got at Vandalia and have spent it all. . . . I have nothing to pay the debt with, and no way to make any money." Lincoln had achieved some fame and distinction, but little in the way of fortune. Material possessions and wants had always meant little to him; after all, all of his life he had gone without. But he had little to show for his political rise. All of his money was go-ing to offset his "national debt." He murmured to Butler, "I don't know what to do."[45]

But by the time he arrived home, Lincoln had come to a decision. His ambitions had now outgrown the confines of the once-thriving New Salem. Any hope that steamboats might navigate the Sangamon River and pass through the village had waned. Residents were mov-ing on to towns with more opportunity. Lincoln had launched his political career in New Salem, but greener pastures beckoned to him too. He collected his few possessions and set his sights on Springfield, where he had developed political associations as a representative from Sangamon County, and where his efforts in the state capital removal project had won him acclaim. His friend John Stuart already enjoyed a flourishing law practice in Springfield, and he invited Lincoln to join him as junior partner. Now twenty-eight years old, Lincoln borrowed a horse, bid fond farewells to his friends and neighbors, stuffed all he owned into his two saddlebags, and rode off.

One of the first people Lincoln encountered in Springfield became one of his closest friends. Joshua Fry Speed came from a wealthy slave-owning family in Kentucky before the enterprising twenty-one-year-old decided to break from his father in 1835. He was one of the many who in this time abandoned roots to try fortunes in the promising prairie lands of Illinois. While opening a general store in Springfield in 1836, Speed first heard Lincoln in a campaign stump and they may have had a brief conversation at that time. On April 15, 1837, Lincoln wandered into Speed's store seeking a mattress and some bedding. He had, according to Speed, "no earthly goods" except for "a pair of saddle-bags, two or three law books, and some clothing." Lincoln's debt so shackled him that he had no money to pay the seventeen dollars for the bedding. "I can never repay you," Lincoln muttered so gloomily that Speed recalled, "I felt for him." Speed offered to share his second-floor room to which Lincoln jumped upstairs, threw down his bags, bounded downstairs, and exclaimed, "'Well Speed I'm moved." The two became lifelong friends and shared the room for the next three years.[46]

Lincoln's new hometown claimed nearly two thousand residents in 1837. Larger and more refined than New Salem, Springfield was still a frontier town, where hogs roamed freely in the streets. Heavy rains left unpaved roads so muddy, dangerous, and odorous that it became the object of ridicule.[47] The manners of the townspeople had not yet reached civility. As John Hay noted, the village combined "the meanness of the North with the barbarism of the South."[48] Lincoln often relayed a joke about Springfield that he credited to Jesse Dubois. The story went that a preacher asked Dubois for permission to use the Hall of Representatives in the new capitol building for a lecture on the second coming of Christ. Dubois responded to him that he spoke nonsense, for "if Christ had been to Springfield once, and got away, he'd be damned clear of coming again."[49]

But other aspects of Springfield proved inviting, especially to younger people seeking cultural and social mobility. An academy, several private schools, and churches dotted the small city. It offered a thespian society, a temperance society, and a lyceum for young men. Its residents could enjoy music, lectures, and amusements not found in most other Illinois communities of the time. After the capital moved to Springfield, legislators, lawyers, judges, and lobbyists congregated there, and along with their wives and daughters brought the town to life.[50] Prominent citizens and socialites lived there including Ninian W. Edwards, son of the former governor; his wife Elizabeth, a member of the prominent Todd family of Kentucky; as well as James Conkling and John Stuart.[51] Certainly Springfield held the markings of a town on the rise. A gentleman in Springfield in March 1837 noted, "It is five years since I visited it [Springfield], and the changes within that period are like the work of enchantment. Flourishing towns . . . farms . . . steam-mills and manufacturing erected, in a country in which the hardy pioneer had at that time sprinkled a few log cabins."[52]

Lincoln's new law partnership with Stuart proved successful, and he found a place to hang his hat. Yet Lincoln felt lonely and depressed in the "busy wilderness" of Springfield. He missed Mary Owens, but painfully aware of his poverty and inability to provide for her, he shrugged off any thought of bringing her there. He penned a letter to her in early May 1837, writing, "This thing of living in Springfield is rather a dull business after all, at least it is so to me. I am quite as lonesome here as [I] ever was anywhere in my life."[53] He admitted that he lacked "any of the polish so important in society life."[54] His deficiency of social graces and still low social standing among Springfield's elite made him uncomfortable. In an era where men of genteel society were expected to be formal, complimentary, and deferential, Lincoln did not fit in. "I should not know how to behave myself," he lamented to Mary Owens.[55]

In regards to his appearance Lincoln did himself no favors either. An acquaintance described him as "awkward, homely, and badly dressed," adding that "although he then had considerable ambition to rise in the world, he had . . . done very little to improve his manners, or appearance, or conversation."[56] But if uncouth, uncultured, and ill groomed, by late 1837 invitations to high-society functions began to float his way. The legislator-lawyer saw these social events as political opportunities as well. Having wealthy friends and connections could certainly come in useful for a rising state politician.

Delving into his law practice, Lincoln began a routine he would keep for the bulk of the next twenty years. His profession as an attorney and later as a circuit-riding lawyer provided dividends for Lincoln. His new law career enlarged his reputation and sharpened his skills of persuasion. Court days provided much hustle and bustle in the county seats, and the visiting attorneys were looked upon almost like celebrities. Lincoln met many new people in the towns across the countryside and built personal alliances with the judges and other lawyers, most of whom had political careers or aspirations. After hours he could be found swapping jokes or engaging in discussions at the local taverns, learning from the locals what political issues concerned them.

Lincoln's legal work halted in July 1837 when Governor Duncan called an emergency special session of the legislature. Duncan needed the legislature to consider whether to officially suspend the charter of the State Bank at Springfield after the bank found itself unable to redeem its loans in gold and silver specie. The governor also recommended a repeal of the gargantuan internal improvements system adopted just months earlier because the state was experiencing difficulty selling enough bonds and securing necessary loans to pay for the projects.[57]

The Panic of 1837—the nation's first economic depression—spurred Duncan's urgency. Indeed, the first half of the 1830s saw a boom time in America. The selling of western lands prompted speculators to overvalue property, and the Bank of the United States lent specie loans to speculators with very few lending restraints. Southern cotton export prices were high, and the country reaped profits from tariffs on imports. In Illinois, land values and lending credit reached an all-time high. All added to good times. However, by 1836, a series of events occurred and the bubble burst. British banks, feeling their own panic, stopped pumping money into the American economy, which slowed their imports of cotton. American banks likewise stopped their loans when the money dried up. Next, Andrew Jackson's 1836 Specie Circu-lar policy of "hard money" supplanted the easy credit–paper money system, meaning that now money had to be paid in gold and silver, which also slowed the money in circulation. After Jackson refused to recharter the Bank of the United States, national bank deposits were removed, sending economic shockwaves across the country. Loans were recalled, interest rates were raised, and investment slowed. Credit and money grew scarce, and land values that had been so high just months before now plummeted. All these factors led to a panic that abruptly stopped the engine of economic progress.[58]

Blaming the crisis on former president Jackson for his closing of the national bank, Duncan convened the legislature to form a response. "Never was wisdom above to direct your counsels more to be implored than at this moment," he implored the legislators.[59] Since little revenue now flowed into the state coffers, the governor saw no other option than to suspend the state banks, revoke their charters, and release the $1,055,604 in state funds held by the banks. With the decreased revenue, Duncan also explicitly urged the legislature to abandon the celebrated internal improvements projects passed months earlier. He previously applauded internal improvements to bolster the state's economic might. But now, with the revenue gone to fund the projects and a debt staring the state in the face, the governor coined the internal improvement system as "evil," and pleaded with the legislators to forfeit the projects.[60]

So on July 1, 1837, Lincoln made the trip to Vandalia. A new face from Sangamon County joined him. Dan Stone had resigned, and in a special election voters elected Edward Baker to replace him. Acquaintances knew Baker, who had been born in England, to be enterprising, ambitious, and able. He had a remarkable penchant for remembering names and faces, a true asset in politics. William Herndon described Baker's emotional oratorical style as "rich and florid and musical."[61] Baker and Lincoln became easy friends, so much so that Lincoln would later name his son Eddie after Baker.

Upon taking their seats, the legislature set to work immediately debating the Bank of Illinois. Lincoln, along with the majority of the legislature, held that if the bank charters were disbanded, it would endanger crucial loans that the Illinois and Michigan Canal and other internal improvements depended upon for revenue.[62] Lincoln also opposed a move that would have held stockholders and bank officers responsible for bank debts. It failed by one vote.[63]

The General Assembly heard the governor's warning about the dire fiscal situation. Some of the internal improvement projects that had already begun now halted because of lack of funding. To add to the troubles, reports of mismanagement from the project engineers and commissioners cast a dark cloud over the whole system. As a result, worried representatives introduced a bill to repeal the entire internal improvements act. But the temptation that Illinois could reach the status of such economically fruitful states as New York proved too strong. Instead, the legislature—with Lincoln among the pack—dissented from the governor and unwisely pushed for *further* internal improvements. Lincoln and others supported measures to proceed with the current surveys and construction, and voiced support for measures that added another $800,000 in internal improvements expenditures.[64] Interestingly, as an attorney for a few companies who held construction contracts, Lincoln sought collection on their behalf for projects, some of which now stood uncompleted.[65]

While bank and internal improvements issues dominated the session, Archer Herndon introduced a bill written by Lincoln to give authority to Springfield to expand its city limits at its discretion, and to give them the power to tax property within the city. The purpose of the bill was to allow Springfield to develop itself for the impending move of the state capital.[66] The *Vandalia Register* reported that $700 in state funds were allocated toward dismantling the Vandalia statehouse, where the cornerstone had just been laid for the new building months prior. The earmarking of those funds prompted the newspaper to wonder why that money couldn't be directed to rehabbing the current site instead of wasting money taking it down.[67]

While other issues required legislators' more immediate attention, Lincoln had yet to make good on the county division. His inability to secure a new county—along with his move to Springfield—did not sit well with some New Salem residents. Some of them felt betrayed, saying they had higher regard for "Abe's smartness than . . .

his honesty." Resident John Potter remembered, "When Abe ran for the legislature . . . the division was the big question. We elected Abe on the Whig ticket. . . . Well, he put our petition in his pocket and didn't do anything for us. . . . Folks felt pretty sore about the way Lincoln did. He never came back here to live, but settled in Springfield and practiced law."⁶⁸

Elsewhere in Sangamon County though, citizens showered accolades on Lincoln and the Long Nine for their efforts, especially in regard to the relocation of the capital to Springfield. In August 1837, the community of Athens held a banquet honoring Lincoln and his colleagues where Lincoln was toasted as "one of nature's nobility." Lincoln responded in appreciation, saying, "Sangamon County will ever be true to her best interests and never more so than in reciprocating the good feelings of the citizens of Athens and neighborhood."⁶⁹ Likewise, citizens in Springfield organized a public dinner to honor their legislators "for a faithful performance of their official duties."⁷⁰ They cheered "the Long Nine of old Sangamon—well done good and faithful servants."⁷¹ They paid tribute to Lincoln, saying, "He fulfilled the expectations of his friends, and disappointed the hopes of his enemies." And Lincoln humbly responded, "All our friends: they are too numerous to mention now individually, while there is not one of them who is not too dear to be forgotten or neglected."⁷²

If Lincoln would not forget his friends, he still felt little impulse to restrain attacks against political foes. During the summer of 1837 while still in legislative session, Lincoln became involved in a legal imbroglio that was marred by partisan motivations. Right before leaving for Vandalia, attorney Lincoln was hired in a lawsuit against James Adams, who Lincoln claimed fraudulently obtained land from a widow after her husband died. It so happened that Adams was running in an upcoming election for probate judge against Dr. Anson Henry, a Whig friend of Lincoln's. The Whigs, intent on defeating Adams, used the lawsuit to smear him. A series of anonymous letters published in the *Sangamo Journal* accused Adams of forging the title to another piece of land that he lived on and alleged that he had stolen it from a man named Sampson. The anonymous letters bore the signature of "Sampson's Ghost," and Lincoln probably wrote them while attending to legislative duties in Vandalia. Adams did not take it lying down, and replied with his own series of letters published in the Sangamon County Democratic newspaper, the *Illinois Republican* (later the *Illinois State Register*). Adams claimed innocence and charged that the slanderous accusations hurled at him were the work of "a knot of Whig lawyers." He rebuked Lincoln personally, calling him a deist. Then, just days before the election between Adams and Henry, Whigs responded by circulating a handbill, likely also written by Lincoln, further detailing allegations against Adams.[73]

Adams enjoyed the last laugh, sailing to a comfortable victory over Henry. Soon after, Lincoln's association with the "Sampson's Ghost" letters was revealed. Despite accusations against him, Adams never faced trial.[74] Lincoln and his Whig friends further attempted to smear Adams after the election by exposing in the *Sangamo* Journal a previous indictment against him for the forgery of deed records in New York.[75] If indeed Adams had engaged in illegal practices, Lincoln, as a lawyer, erred in trying the case in the court of public opinion rather than the court of law. He acted recklessly, and unfortunately continued to use newspaper attacks against political opponents. Only after the "Rebecca letters" against state auditor James Shields in 1842—at least one of which may have been contributed by Lincoln—did Lincoln cease the practice of political smears. Lincoln's character, by this time, had manifestly developed and matured, but he had not yet learned how to moderate his partisan ambitions.

Lincoln did not confine such imprudence to political letter writing. Lincoln's sometimes-graceless tactics showed in his romantic relationships as well. Shortly after returning from the July 1837 session, Lincoln began to have second thoughts about a commitment to Mary Owens. In a half-hearted attempt to wriggle out of his engagement with her, Lincoln wrote to her stating, "I want in all cases to do right, and most particularly so, in all cases with women. I want, at this particular time, more than anything else, to do right with you." Rather than speak to her in person, Lincoln awkwardly broke the relationship via letter, bluntly offering, "I am now willing to release you." He concluded by stating, "If it suits you best to not answer this—farewell—a long life and a merry one attend you." He signed, "Your friend, Lincoln."[76] Not surprisingly, she did not write him back, and that terminated the relationship.

On the legislative front, Lincoln watched in horror as the economic crisis in the nation deepened. "One loud, deep, uninterrupted groan of hard times is echoed from one end of the country to another," the *Sangamo Journal* bemoaned. In Illinois, loans stopped, credit could not be obtained, and the Bank of Illinois at Springfield and the Bank of Shawneetown suspended specie payments, which put them in jeopardy for automatic forfeiture of their charters.[77]

Meanwhile, the slavery issue resounded full force in Illinois in November 1837. In the town of Alton a proslavery mob set fire to the warehouse belonging to newspaperman Elijah Lovejoy. A Presbyterian minister and ardent abolitionist, Lovejoy had moved to the free state of Illinois from Missouri in early 1837 to open the abolitionist newspaper the *Alton Observer.* He rebuked slavery, and railed against the church's and the North's complicity in slavery. Lovejoy soon found that Illinois did not tolerate abolitionism. The *Sangamo Journal,* as with most newspapers, admonished the influence of abolitionists, writing that "efforts of abolitionists in this community are neither necessary nor useful," and their demands for immediate emancipation "are at variance with Christianity." Adding fuel to the fire, the Illinois Antislavery Convention decided to meet in Lovejoy's hometown of Alton in October of 1837. Residents in Alton reacted in anger to Lovejoy's efforts, and three times destroyed his printing press. He refused to back down. In November, the vengeful mob claimed his press for the final time and finally his life. Abolitionists hailed Lovejoy as a martyr.[78]

How to reconcile the incendiary issues of slavery and abolition within the realm of law weighed on Lincoln's mind. While still not sympathetic to abolitionist aims, Lincoln had taken a stand in the legislature earlier in the year against prohibiting abolitionist societies. Just days following that January 1837 vote in the legislature, Lincoln received an invitation to speak at the Young Men's Lyceum in Springfield to be held in January 1838. The Lyceum—the brainchild of a group of young politicos that included John T. Stuart and Dan Stone—formed in 1833 as a vehicle for young idealists to advance and exchange ideas. By 1838, it held a place as a leading cultural activity in Springfield.[79] Lyceum organizers allowed Lincoln to choose the topic of his speech. It would afford him the largest audience he had yet commanded. Not coincidentally, the timing of the Lyceum invitation and the state legislative vote on abolitionism merged, prompting Lincoln to write a speech on how to respond to slavery and abolition in legal and moral terms. He might have been expected to select as a lyceum topic the economic panic facing the nation, or how the state needed to stay the course on the bank and internal improvements, or the need to advance Whig partisan causes. Rather, fresh off the November murder of Lovejoy, Lincoln felt the impetus to attempt to frame how the American republic should effectively deal with law and order. By doing so he hoped to raise public consciousness concerning increased mob activity in civil society.

With the title, "The Perpetuation of Our Political Institutions," Lincoln warned of the "approach of danger" in the country hailing not from abroad, but rather "amongst us." He proceeded to lay out the case that an undeniable and increasing disregard for the law in the form of mob action had begun to pervade the country. Though he did not mention Lovejoy by name, Lincoln referred to the recent shooting of the printing press editor and other incidents as prime examples of the "lawless spirit" in the republic. In stark terms he cast the situation: "Whenever the vicious portion of population shall be permitted to gather in bands of hundreds and thousands, and burn churches, ravage and rob provision stores, throw printing presses into rivers, shoot editors, and hang and burn obnoxious persons at pleasure, and with impunity; depend on it, this Government cannot last." He further lamented, "If destruction be our lot, we must ourselves be its author and finisher. As a nation of freemen, we must live through all time, or die by suicide."[80]

Lincoln's answer to that problem: "Let reverence for the laws . . . become the political religion of the nation." Rather than resort to passion, he argued submission to law and to reason. "Reason, cold, calculating, unimpassioned reason," he offered, "must furnish all the materials for our future support and defense." While not surprising to hear an attorney embrace reverence for the law, it underscored the degree to which self-restraint and respect for the law underlay Lincoln's view of a functioning republic.[81] To some extent, rowdy frontier culture spawned mob activity and lawlessness. It had become a by-product of the Jacksonian democracy movement, in which people thought that liberties afforded them the right to conduct themselves how they wished, rather than submitting to legal restraints.[82]

Lincoln took the notion of restraint a step further, stating, "Towering genius disdains a beaten path. It seeks regions hitherto unexplored." While this can be viewed as a lofty encouragement to those seeking to advance in the world, he meant it just the opposite as a warning to keep ambitions in check, and to work for the common good rather than for one's own benefit and promotion. The ambition to achieve a pinnacle of towering genius, if left unchecked, could be dire to oneself and to society. He concluded that a search for towering genius leaves people never satisfied. "It scorns to tread in the footsteps of any predecessor, however illustrious. It thirsts and burns for distinction."[83] While there were certainly political opponents to whom that statement applied, Lincoln may well have had himself in mind. He long held that he wished to render himself worthy of the respect of others. Now that he had gained acclaim, how much burning for distinction accompanied it?

Throughout his legislative career, Lincoln, in the words of one who knew him, "was seized with political aspirations."[84] Friend Ward Hill Lamon likewise observed Lincoln's "thirst for distinction." Lamon held that this thirst "governed all his conduct," and became the "great object of his life."[85] "He was ambitious seeking position," noted Springfield physician William Jayne. In Jayne's perspective, Lincoln sought ambition not for self-gain but with the goal of "expecting to benefit his country."[86] But Albert Bledsoe, who met Lincoln in 1838 right after he moved to Springfield, detected other motives behind Lincoln's thirst for distinction. Bledsoe later asserted, in a less than complimentary tone, that "when he [Lincoln] was a candidate himself, he thought the whole canvass . . . ought to be conducted with reference to *his* success" (emphasis added). Bledsoe bluntly called Lincoln a "cold, calculating reasoner," whose "ruling passion," "political thirst for distinction," and "eagerness for power," drove him with such intensity that he "used men as tools . . . to feed *his* desires" (emphasis added).[87] In Bledsoe's opinion, in the attempt to win the esteem of his fellow man, "popularity was Mr. Lincoln's idol."[88] Bledsoe did state this years later after having been an anti-Lincoln Confederate sympathizer, but that in itself does not disqualify Bledsoe's assessment as unreliable or inaccurate.

Lincoln hoped the Lyceum address might raise his social standing. It would be published in newspapers and would be much talked about. The flowery verbosity of his speech was intended to impress the elite, who still saw Lincoln as a country politician and lawyer. In florid prose, he describes the tides of history as "a forest of giant oaks" which had been "despoiled of its verdure, shorn of its foliage; unshading and unshaded, to murmur in a few gentle breezes."[89] Friends called the address "bombastic" and "sophomoric."[90] But Lincoln ignored such derision. He had already mastered the art of stump speaking to the rural masses. Perhaps this speech to the Lyceum would elevate his reputation.

THE PRIZE AND PRICE OF POLITICS

On February 24, 1838, Lincoln decided to stand for a third term as state representative. He released to the *Sangamo Journal* his announcement: "We are authorized to announce A. LINCOLN, as a candidate for the State Legislature."[1] Having now served two terms, Lincoln did not need to write up a platform as he had before. He did attend several joint meetings for voters (as he had in 1836) throughout the county, to which all seventeen candidates for the legislature were invited. When his circuit work allowed it, he hit the campaign trail. He did so not for himself but for his friend and law partner, John Stuart, who again sought a seat in Congress. Stephen Douglas challenged Stuart for the seat, and the partisan war began. In a poke at Douglas's height, Lincoln wrote wryly to fellow Whig representative William Minshall of Schuyler County, "We have adopted it as part of our policy here, to never speak of Douglas at all. Isn't that the best mode of treating so small a matter?"[2]

But Lincoln undoubtedly considered Douglas more than a "small matter." He had squared off against Douglas on the other side of the legislative aisle, so he knew of Douglas's abilities. In February 1838, Lincoln wrote a series of letters to the *Sangamo Journal* signed "the Conservative," charging that Douglas and his Democratic ideas were out of touch with the district. Thereafter the campaign turned bitter and malicious. In the back of Speed's store, which had become a local gathering spot, Stuart and Douglas became embroiled in a shouting match. On another occasion, after Stuart lambasted Douglas

Pay voucher for service in legislature, 1838. This voucher for a hundred dollars to Abraham Lincoln served as his pay for half of the 1838–39 session. He received four dollars per day plus a travel allowance. Courtesy of Lincoln Heritage Museum.

in a speech in Springfield, Douglas grabbed Stuart by the neck and paraded him around the crowd. Stuart got free of Douglas's grip by biting the Little Giant so hard on the hand that Douglas bore tooth marks on his thumb for the rest of his life.[3]

Stuart held such confidence in Lincoln that he allowed him to debate the popular Douglas as his proxy.[4] So on several occasions throughout the congressional district in 1838 Lincoln and Douglas debated, a precursor to their infamous contest as candidates for the U.S. Senate twenty years later. Usher Linder recalled the "Little Giant" Stephen Douglas and the formidably tall Abraham Lincoln frequently pitted against each other, noting that "they both commanded marked attention and respect."[5] Lincoln's involvement had helped, as Stuart squeaked out a narrow victory in late September, defeating Douglas by a mere thirty-six votes from a total 36,495 cast.[6]

In his own legislative race, Lincoln sailed to victory for a third time on August 6, 1838. At 1,803 votes he again polled the highest vote total of all the candidates from the county. Whigs Ninian Edwards, Edward Baker, William Elkin, and Andrew McCormick also won seats, as did Lincoln's former surveying partner, Democrat John Calhoun.[7] Robert Wilson lost likely because his home area of Petersburg resented his compromising stance on county division. That Lincoln had likewise not succeeded in securing county division did not seem to affect his popularity, though his support in Democratic New Salem did diminish from 1836.[8]

When the Eleventh General Assembly convened on December 3, 1838, it would be the final time that Vandalia would serve as the state capital. The complexion of this legislature reflected less change than previous sessions. The legislative accomplishments of the previous legislature handed victory to incumbents. For the first time, experienced members were more numerous than new ones. Demonstrating their increasing electoral success, the Whig Party found themselves in the majority for the first time. They backed their new favorite son Abraham Lincoln for House Speaker. Unfortunately for Lincoln, several Whigs were absent when the Speaker vote took place. Additionally, an internal party rift, largely a result of the capital removal vote, upended his chances for the speakership. On the fourth ballot, William Ewing, now back in the state legislature after a recent stint as U.S. senator, prevailed by just six votes. Lincoln took over as Whig floor leader again. He received two committee assignments: the Finance Committee and the Committee on Counties.[9]

As the transfer of a new governor occurred, outgoing governor Duncan implored the legislature to discard the internal improvements programs entirely. With the crisis upon the state, nearly two million dollars had been spent with little evidence of progress.[10] The new governor, Macoupin County Democrat Thomas Carlin, took a more positive tone. He promoted a common school system, touted the Illinois and Michigan Canal project, and supported state banks, declaring that it would be a "suicidal policy" to abolish them.[11] Above all, Carlin repudiated Duncan and encouraged the state legislature to carry on with the internal improvement system, saying too much had already been invested to turn back.[12]

But then, the state auditor released his report in December of 1838 showing that the state's ending balance for the year stood at just ninety-two dollars. Worse yet, expenses were predicted to outpace revenue.[13] Some assemblymen sweated the news and began to shrink back from the costly internal improvement ventures. But Lincoln—the "DeWitt Clinton of Illinois"—did not concur. A piece written in the *Sangamo Journal* by "the Citizen," likely authored by Lincoln, appealed to workingmen, declaring that the projects have raised the spirits "of many a farmer and mechanic."[14] Lincoln agreed with Carlin about not turning back. He remarked in an impassioned speech on the House floor: "We are now so far advanced in a general system of internal improvements that, if we would, we cannot retreat from it, without disgrace and great loss."[15] He vowed that "his limbs should be torn before he violated that pledge."[16] To Lincoln, the only logical conclusion was, "We must advance."[17] He earnestly believed that if the state would confidently ride out the panic, the economy would rebound and the projects could continue unabated. He also felt bound somewhat to those counties who had been promised projects in return for their support of the capital relocation.[18] According to the *Vandalia Free Press,* Lincoln professed that "Sangamon County had received great and important benefits, at the last session of the Legislature, in return for giving support, thro' her delegation to the system of Internal Improvement." Thus "she is morally bound, to adhere to that system, through all time to come!"[19]

The Long Nine, however, no longer were of one mind on that matter. The internal improvements debacle began to divide the ranks. According to a Vandalia newspaper, one evening after session, Baker and Lincoln had a heated exchange over internal improvements. After Baker reported himself now against the system, Lincoln replied coarsely that every representative of Sangamon County present and future must support the system because of how they obtained the seat of government in Springfield, saying the pledge was "forever binding."[20]

A north-south state divide also crept into the legislature over internal improvements. Part of the dissension stemmed from the southern Illinois prejudice that incoming "Yankee" settlers were dishonest, money-hungry industrialists. But southern Illinois also depended upon the completion of the Illinois Central Railroad commencing from Cairo, and they feared being drowned out by a growing northern Illinois majority. W. J. Gatewood of Gallatin County threatened that if northern Illinoisans pulled the plug on internal improvements including the railroad, he would see to it that the Illinois and Michigan Canal be killed as well.[21]

But rather than supporting only the continuation of projects already in the pipeline, Lincoln unwisely joined the effort for more *new* projects. These included his support for bills providing for a railroad to Carlinville from Alton and Shelbyville, for an additional $50,000 to be added to a $100,000 appropriation for an improvement to the Rock River, and a $20,000 Big Muddy River improvement.[22] These latest plans had no complete surveys of the rivers or the lands upon which roads would be built, and no hard cost estimates.[23]

Payment options for the state government's bills were few. Selling more state bonds proved tricky in such an anxious economic climate, so Lincoln offered a scheme. His Finance Committee forwarded a resolution proposing that the state buy twenty million acres of unsold public land from the federal government for twenty-five cents per acre then resell the land at $1.25 per acre. He figured it would be enough to pay off the debt, cover interest due, and cover the costs of the committed internal improvement projects. The resolution passed, but Congress did not act on it.[24] Lincoln urged the legislature not to give up on the projects. He claimed that like a steam engine the state was difficult to turn around, but once it did so all would again be well.[25]

Even if the land sale scheme would work, no immediate revenue would be realized. Legislators proposed an alternative: a revenue bill imposing a state tax of twenty-five cents per one hundred dollars of assessed value on all property in the state. Previously, only property of nonresidents was subject to state taxation, and property taxes on residents went solely into county treasuries for county purposes. This would be the first state tax applied to all landowners in the state, so this revenue bill invited a storm of protest, but it passed. Lincoln voted in favor of the bill, and explained his rationale in a letter to a Bond County citizen concerned about the new revenue law. Lincoln reasoned that as the state population increased, so did financial demands on the state. He also contended that since the law taxed land according to its value, it would take from the "*wealthy few*" rather than the "*many poor*" (his emphasis). Even if the wealthy few thought the tax unfair, he continued, they were "not sufficiently numerous to carry the elections."[26] It's tempting to conclude from this that Lincoln supported a progressive taxation system. But Lincoln's support

PUBLIC LANDS IN ILLINOIS.

JANUARY 17, 1839.

Read, laid on the table, and ordered to be printed.

Mr. LINCOLN, from the Committee on Finance, made the following

REPORT:

The Committee on Finance, to which was referred a resolution of this House instructing them to inquire into the expediency of proposing to purchase of the Government of the United States all the unsold lands lying within the limits of the State of Illinois, have had the same under consideration, and report:

That, in their opinion, if such purchase could be made on reasonable terms, two objects of high importance to the State might thereby be effected—first, acquire control over all the territory within the limits of the State—and, second, acquire an important source of revenue.

We will examine these two points in their order, and with special reference to their bearing upon our internal improvement system.

In the first place, then, we are now so far advanced in a general system of internal improvements that, if we would, we cannot retreat from it without disgrace and great loss. The conclusion then is, that we *must* advance; and, if so, the first reason for the State acquiring title to the public land is, that while we are at great expense in improving the country, and thereby enhancing the value of all the real property within its limits, that enhancement may attach exclusively to property owned by *ourselves* as a State, or to its citizens as individuals, and *not* to that owned by the Government of the United States. Again, it is conceded every where, as we believe, that Illinois surpasses every other spot of equal extent upon the face of the globe, in *fertility* of soil, and in the proportionable amount of the same which is sufficiently level for actual cultivation; and consequently that she is endowed by nature with the capacity of sustaining a greater amount of agricultural wealth and population than any other equal extent of territory in the world. To such an amount of wealth and population, our internal improvement system, now so alarming, in view of its having to be borne by our present numbers, and with our present means, would be a burden of no sort of consequence. How important, then, is it that all our energies should be exerted to bring that wealth and population among us as speedily as possible. But what, it may be asked, can the ownership of the land by the State do towards the accomplishment of that desirable object? It may be answered that the chief obstruction to the more rapid settlement of our country is found in for the Revenue Law was merely pragmatic—a necessary move to erase the state's revenue shortfall. Not all agreed. The legislature had previously assured citizens that no taxes would be needed to fund the state's budget, and Senator Browning, among others, worried that this act would be the first step toward a state "crushed by taxation."[27]

While debates over revenue ensued, representatives partial to Vandalia still refused to admit defeat over the capital relocation passed in the previous session. Representative William Lee Ewing announced his intention to introduce "an act to repeal certain laws relative to the permanent location of the seat of Government of the State of Illinois."[28] Ewing's agenda was personal. He had campaigned in 1838 on a promise "to be a thorn in the sides of the Long Nine," and now wanted to make good on that vow.[29] In a harsh and stirring speech on the House floor he denounced the "arrogance of Springfield" in its claim to the seat of government. While not a new charge, he leveled accusations of "chicanery," and said that the Sangamon delegation "sold out the internal improvement men" in exchange for "their support to every measure that would gain them a vote to the law removing the seat of government."[30]

Lincoln would not be backed into a corner by Ewing. He responded to the offensives with severity, charging that Ewing's allegations were unbecoming a proper statesman. Lincoln put on such a show that even Usher Linder recalled that "this was the first time that I began to conceive a very high opinion of the talent and personal courage of Abraham Lincoln."[31] The debate turned fervid. The prideful Ewing shot up, and directing his words to the Sangamon County delegation furiously inquired, "Gentlemen, have you no other champion than this course and vulgar fellow?" and stood ready to duel Lincoln. Colleagues coaxed Ewing away from the challenge.[32]

Raising Ewing's ire further, in early January 1839, Lincoln moved to appropriate $128,300 to complete the new statehouse in Springfield. He made sure that the Senate passed the appropriation bill first to make it easier to pass the House. Ewing joined William Hankins of Fayette and Orlando Ficklin of Coles in an attempt to forestall the appropriation, arguing that in the face of debt all such funds should come from private individuals. Hankins proposed the formation of a commission to locate a new capital site. Peter Green of Clay then moved that any appropriation be subject to a public vote. All measures were defeated. Lincoln became greatly frustrated by all of the stonewalling tactics, writing to John Stuart that Ewing "is not worth a damn."[33] Lincoln decided to be equally stubborn by moving that all legislative business be postponed so that the House could take up the Senate appropriation bill. His motion met with defeat when the House voted instead to adjourn for the rest of the day. But in the end, his fight to hold the capital in Springfield succeeded when the very next day, the House approved the appropriation bill.[34]

Meanwhile the issue of county division polarized the citizens of Sangamon. Lincoln knew his constituents' wishes should be heeded but wanted to tread carefully. In January Lincoln presented a protest on behalf of Sangamon County citizens against the apportionment of the county into four parts. He then aided in drawing up a plan for division in which Sangamon would retain the largest land area and population. Referring the bill to the Committee on Counties of which he was a member, Lincoln crafted a bill establishing three new counties from Sangamon: Dane, Menard, and Logan—the latter county he named for Democrat state representative John Logan from Jackson County to help secure votes from Democrats.[35] Fellow Sangamon representative Dawson added an amendment to the bill that the House award $2,000 to each of the new counties of Dane, Menard, and Logan, noting that in another bill that had created Scott County from Morgan, the legislature had awarded Scott $2000. That amendment failed, but in March 1839, thanks to Lincoln's guidance, a division bill finally made it through the General Assembly, and because of its still relative size, Sangamon County kept five representative seats.[36] It would be another feather in Lincoln's legislative cap.

In the midst of other legislative duties in 1839, Lincoln stepped in to resolve a skirmish between fellow representative Edward Baker and Lincoln's friend from New Salem William Butler. The rift started when Butler wrote to Baker accusing the Sangamon County representatives of drawing new county boundary lines favoring certain petitioners' wishes. Both were Lincoln's friends, so to make amends Lincoln wrote a series of letters to Butler, excusing Baker but also defending himself against allegations that had also targeted him. Lincoln vehemently denied in the letter that he had been "bought up" by the parties whom Butler named: John Taylor, who had actively led the petitioners to establish the new county of Menard; and John Wright and George W. Turley, both of Mount Pulaski, who were active petitioners for the new county of Logan.[37] "Are you not ashamed of writing such a letter as that?" Lincoln asked Butler curtly. "If you believe the charges you make to be true, I say most flatly you are a fool."[38] Lincoln clarified the manner in which the county lines were drawn, disavowing any notions of treachery or duplicity, and denying that he was "capable of betraying my friends for any price."[39] Lincoln and Baker's responses may have not settled Butler's qualms but the tension abated. Butler wrote to Baker later in the month that "it was not my intention to insult you or any one of my friends."[40] Butler even offered Lincoln the use of a horse to come back to Springfield when the session ended.

With each passing legislative session, the chasm in the legislature along party lines grew more evident. To rally support behind President Van Buren and the heroic Old Hickory, Democrats in early January announced an anniversary celebration in honor of Jackson's victory at the battle of New Orleans to be held at a Vandalia tavern. Invitations were sent out to "the true friends of the late and present administration."[41] Likewise, the following month Whigs officially opened their 1840 presidential campaign at an evening meeting in Vandalia. Lincoln stated that the meeting's purpose would be so that "all the opponents of misrule" of the Jackson and Van Buren administrations could "unite upon the common platform of Union and compromise."[42]

The partisan shadow hung over numerous legislative debates as well, particularly with the bank battle. Democratic opponents of the state bank renewed their efforts to quash the bank and revoke its charter. For several days on end in January the House fought over various resolutions concerning an independent federal treasury and of the rechartering of the Bank of the United States, issues that the state had no control over. Jackson had crushed the bank, but the Panic of 1837 left President Van Buren in a quandary. Funds from the national bank had been entrusted to state banks across the country. Van Buren didn't necessarily believe that the state banks were unsafe depositories for federal funds, but did believe that some were poorly managed and desired more bank safeguards. He advocated an independent treasury system—a sort of subtreasury that would separate funds from state banks that would be monitored by an independent federal treasury. The president envisioned that this subtreasury would be responsible for the collection and disbursement of public revenue, and would not be used for unchecked credit lending and speculation, which had in part led to the Panic of 1837. The hope would be that the subtreasury would serve as the mechanism to regulate the nation's economy. Congress became mired in conflict over the subtreasury idea, and it trickled down to the states.[43]

Largely because the creation of a subtreasury would directly affect the fate of state banks, the Illinois legislature debated the issue hotly. Illinois Democrats largely supported their president and wrote resolutions in favor of the independent subtreasury, calling upon Congress to vote for it. The Whigs responded in kind, calling the resolutions "injudicious, inexpedient and unwise."[44] Lincoln chided the subtreasury idea as a "scheme of fraud and corruption."[45] Seeing that they would not be able to summon a majority in the House for their resolutions, Whigs took the action to the Senate, forcing the House to vote on the resolutions. For one whole day in January 1839, it became of test of wills, as the House argued the bill from nine o'clock in the morning to dusk. The protracted saga ended with the Democrats admitting defeat. Lincoln proudly boasted of the Whig victory over the Democratic Party "loco-focos"—the derogatory term that the Whigs used against Democrats who abandoned the Jeffersonian and Jacksonian ideal for the elitist Martin Van Buren.[46] Considering that the subtreasury was a federal issue, the Whig "victory" was more a matter of scoring political points rather than securing a meaningful legislative win.

Opponents of the bank again tried to raise doubts as to the solvency and accountability of the state bank. As with the previous session, resolutions were introduced to examine the Bank of Illinois at Springfield and the Bank of Illinois at Shawneetown. The lines of supporters and opponents were drawn again, but this time party lines divided the Sangamon County delegation. Lincoln and Dawson opposed investigation into the state bank, whereas Calhoun, Elkin, and McCormick supported it. Bank supporters successfully tabled that motion. A limited examination was approved, but only to investigate whether the state bank had engaged in the lead trade at Galena or the salt pork trade in Alton without authorization.[47]

Meanwhile, another demonstration of the impact of slavery in the country came before the legislature in early 1839. The governor of Maine had recently declined to extradite two abolitionist citizens of that state accused of kidnapping a Georgia slave. The Illinois House proposed one resolution condemning the governor's actions, and a second resolution affirming that citizens of nonslaveholding states should not interfere with the rights of those in slaveholding states. Lincoln felt inclination to support the measures, but deliberated over the precedent they would set. He made a motion to postpone the subject indefinitely. The House agreed and nothing came of it. The assembly also took up a resolution proposed by John Calhoun declaring that Congress should not abolish slavery in the District of Columbia or prohibit slave trade between states. No action resulted from that resolution either.[48]

Reflecting the changing laws guiding the frontier, Lincoln, in 1839, presented a petition of 631 citizens of Sangamon County "praying the repeal of all laws authorizing the retailing of intoxicating liquors."[49] Nothing came of that bill. Days later two other bills of note came before the legislature: one bill authorizing law enforcement agents to apprehend horse thieves, and another prohibiting betting on elections. Lincoln supported both.[50] He also lent his support to create the "Illinois Asylum for the education of the deaf and dumb."[51] The legislature approved, in early 1839, redrawing judicial boundaries in the state into nine judicial circuits.[52] As a circuit-riding lawyer Lincoln would come to know the eighth judicial circuit quite well.

The General Assembly adjourned on March 4, 1839. The partisan battles, tension between members, and troublesome issues at hand compelled John Hardin to reflect that that the assembly had "a stormy session & a very unpleasant one."[53] It had been an active session for

Lincoln as he voted on 157 of 181 possible roll call votes, and served on eleven select committees.[54] He pocketed $302 for his services, to add to the $100 he received in December, and headed north. The legislature left Vandalia as the city faded into history as the capital. State workers packed state archives into boxes, and loaded them on to wagons in the rain heading north to Lincoln's hometown of Springfield.[55]

On July 4, 1839, Governor Carlin proclaimed Springfield the new capital of Illinois. By now, the town of Springfield contained some twenty-five hundred residents. The new statehouse stood in the public square surrounded by businesses including the Bank of Illinois. The town offered even more now that it welcomed state government. That June, Springfield trustees selected Lincoln to fill a vacancy as town trustee, and he served until the spring of the following year when the city began under a new charter that Lincoln had helped usher through the legislature.[56]

Upon arriving back in Springfield, Lincoln met residents who sternly disagreed with his support for the revenue law that the General Assembly had passed a few months prior. As representatives of the residents, Lincoln, along with Herndon, McCormick, Calhoun, and Edwards, decided it necessary to hold a public meeting for anyone in the county to attend and present their arguments, so that the representatives could demonstrate that "none of [the criticisms] are well founded."[57] Their strategy seemed to quell voter anger.

Lincoln devoted day-to-day activity in 1839 and 1840 to his law practice, but also found time for politics. Central Illinois Whigs expected Stephen Douglas to again challenge John Stuart in the race for U.S. Congress in 1840. The battle between Stuart and Douglas would certainly be another hard-fought battle. Similar to his earlier efforts, Lincoln wrote letters to Whig newspapers across the state to rally the Whig Party faithful.[58]

On a November evening in 1839 in the back room of Joshua Speed's store, the political banter ratcheted up. Among those present were Lincoln, Stephen Douglas, and Speed's employee William Herndon. Douglas and Lincoln began to joust while the others sat transfixed. After several minutes of back and forth, the impetuous and fiery Douglas leaped to his feet and challenged any Whig to publicly debate him. Several ultimately accepted the challenge. So, for the next week in the Springfield Presbyterian Church, orators took turns on the platform. Stephen Douglas, Jesse Thomas, Josiah Lamborn, and John Calhoun represented the Democrats. Edward Baker, Orville Browning, Stephen Logan, and Lincoln took turns upholding the Whig cause.[59] In an era that prized public oratory, the debates must have been quite a spectacle.

Lincoln closed out the debates with a salient speech—using no notes—criticizing Douglas and his support of the subtreasury. Using hyperbolic language he charged the Van Buren administration with robbery and fraud, proclaiming, "I know that the great volcano at Washington, aroused and directed by the evil spirit that reigns there, is belching forth the lava of political corruption, in a current broad and deep, which is sweeping with frightful velocity over the whole length and breadth of the land . . . riding like demons on the waves of Hell . . . taunting all those who dare resist its destroying course."[60] In the spirit of partisan debate, he stooped to political hypocrisy, denouncing Van Buren for excessively contributing to the public debt, ignoring the reality that he had done likewise with the internal improvements projects.[61] Whigs roundly praised the speech that the *Sangamo Journal* printed in pamphlet form, and even Lincoln beamed. "I made a big speech," he crowed to Stuart following the oration, "to enlighten you and the rest of the world."[62]

In November of 1839, Sangamon County voters held a special election to fill a House vacancy following the resignation of John Calhoun. Lincoln had firmly established his stature as a party leader, and that afforded him sway on the party choices in elections. That influence gave the *Illinois State Register* cause to be suspicious of Lincoln's motives, resulting in a partisan mêlée for several weeks leading up to the special election. It started simply enough in early November 1839 when the *Register* wrote that the bank was solely a Whig institution, a charge that Lincoln denied in a written rebuttal in the *Sangamo Journal*.[63] The *Register* then fired back charging "the longest of the long-nine" and his "Springfield Junto" of conspiring to dictate who would fill the House vacancy, announcing that Lincoln preferred candidate John Bennett. The *Register* suspected that

Lincoln would only pick someone who could be a yes man for him. They wrote: "Would Mr. Lincoln be likely to urge a candidate upon the people, unless he were well assured that he would, if elected, go the whole hog with the Springfield Junto members?"[64] An annoyed Lincoln opined that the *Register* lied, saying that his candidate of choice had been his friend Bowling Green, and not Bennett. The *Register* responded that they disliked Lincoln's "game of buffoonery" against the paper.[65] As it happened, neither Green nor Bennett won. The candidates fought closely, but in the end Thomas Nance prevailed. He would be a Sangamon County representative, and the first state representative for the newly formed counties of Logan, Menard, and Dane (the latter county's name changed later to Christian).[66]

In early October 1839, Governor Carlin called for the General Assembly to convene. Work continued on the state capitol when the assembly met in December, so the House met in the Second Presbyterian Church in Springfield. Carlin warned the legislature of the state's rapidly deteriorating economic condition, calling it "alarming." Just as with his predecessor, Carlin had once enthusiastically supported internal improvements but now urged the legislature to suspend operation on those "extravagant," "ruinous," and "destructive" projects, and to concentrate only on the most promising railroads and larger rivers."[67]

Lincoln privately demurred the future of the previous legislative gains. He continued his written correspondence to Stuart in Washington as they discussed cases in their law practice, exchanged updates on progress in their respective legislative bodies, forecasted political changes, and traded ideas on how to bolster chances for the 1840 presidential election. In a January 1840 letter, Lincoln offered a litany of predictions for the session: "The following is my guess as to what will be done. The Internal Improvement System will be put down in a lump, without benefit of clergy. The Bank will be resuscitated with some trifling modifications. Whether the canal will go ahead or stop is verry doubtful." Lincoln even expressed reservations about the new statehouse construction.[68] Indeed, several of his predictions would be accurate.

One of the more peculiar moves in this session involved an attempt by some southern Illinois legislators to eliminate the increasing political concentration of northern Illinois. A House member proposed a bill to cede to Wisconsin the fourteen most northern counties of Illinois. Thankfully, wiser heads—Lincoln's included—prevailed, pointing to the advantages of the growing city of Chicago and its port access on the all-important Lake Michigan. Had the bill succeeded, Chicago would have been in Wisconsin, and Illinois might have been more economically tied to the South, resulting in grave consequences for the future of the state and the nation.[69]

As expected, fiscal issues dominated the discussion of the 1839–40 session. Many legislators felt that the national Specie Act of 1836, which directed that banks should deal only in gold and silver specie and not paper money, had in part triggered the Panic of 1837. They stood uncertain as to whether the state should follow suit or whether to order the bank to suspend specie payments. Lincoln believed the greater availability of paper money better enabled poorer citizens to thrive, but likewise held that specie should still be circulated. His Finance Committee issued a report in December stating that "nothing in this act contained, shall be construed to legalize the suspension of specie payment." That report won the day.[70]

As Lincoln predicted, legislators concerned over internal improvements costs resolved to roll back the imperiled projects. Opponents took a vote to repeal the projects, which Lincoln and the majority narrowly rejected. Weeks later, several resolutions were introduced suspending construction on railroads and river improvements save for one or two select projects, which also met narrow defeat. In an effort to ensure accountability, the House did pass resolutions requiring that commissioners of railroad projects report all expenditures and number of engineers employed, a measure Lincoln supported. Hoping it would stir protest against the projects, internal improvements opponents offered resolutions such as requiring all male inhabitants to work three days a year on public roads. That tactic also failed.[71] Lincoln did raise the sensible motion to form private joint-stock companies to provide capital investment rather than relying on the state's finances. That move led the *Illinois State Register* to mock Lincoln as a "joint stock company man."[72]

To help rescue the faltering internal improvements system, Lincoln took to the House floor. Before a crowded gallery, Lincoln pleaded that the projects should be sustained and were necessary for the state even in the face of debt: "At least some portion of our Internal Improvements should be carried on. That after the immense debt, we have incurred in carrying these works almost to completion, at least one work calculated to yield something towards defraying its expense, should be finished and put in operation."[73] As chairman of the committee for the Illinois and Michigan Canal project, he also lobbied hard for the canal.

Statewide meetings had urged internal improvements in 1836. Now in 1839 similar statewide meetings condemned them. Citizens faulted the legislature for acting "injudiciously and contrary to the best interest of those whom they pretended to represent."[74] The *Illinois State Register* summarized the dilemma: "The people of this county demand the System shall be reduced to the wants of the country, and so changed as to save them from taxation to support and carry it on." Laying the blame at the feet of the Long Nine, the *Register* concluded, "No trifling will be allowed in this matter; for Mr. Lincoln and his associates of the Long Nine will be forced to choose between themselves and their constituents."[75]

The legislature read the public opinion. Seven times in December 1839 and January 1840 the House voted to repeal the extensive projects of 1837, with Lincoln adamantly voting no seven times. Joshua Speed noted that upon deciding a course of action as right, Lincoln rarely retreated from it. The intense hammering of internal improvements began to show results, and as the month of January 1840 wore on, majority support waned. Earlier proponents of internal improvements projects—including the original sponsor of the mammoth system, former representative Stephen Douglas—now denounced the system as "wild and extravagant."[76] Others proudly professed their consistent dissociation, including Orville Browning who boasted, "From the very first moment the bill made its appearance in the Senate, I have been doing battle against it, and I thank God, that in whatever else I may have erred, I have not to atone for the sin of having voted for one solitary measure connected with the whole system."[77]

Near the end of January 1840, the House again took a final vote, and this time, the General Assembly voted the general system of internal improvements of 1837 "hereby repealed," and the board of commissioners and the board of public works "discharged and dismissed" from duties.[78] All contractors were to be paid for the work done, and all unsold bonds were to be returned and destroyed. The *Chicago Republican* flashed in all capital letters: "DESTRUCTION OF THE SYSTEM."[79]

Unwavering to the end, Lincoln voted no on all repeal attempts. Extremely disappointed by the action of the legislature, he took his $228 check and cut out early; he was absent from the legislature when it adjourned on February 5, 1840.[80]

Through it all, Lincoln had again proven to be among the most skillful in the legislature. Respect and admiration from his colleagues had grown tremendously. But while he demonstrated steadfastness, he supposed that his support for taxation and for the state bank as well as his ardent stance behind the internal improvements projects in the face of mounting state debt might cost him politically. He would be up for re-election again in 1840, but could he even win again? Reflecting on his chances for re-election, he frankly admitted to Stuart in a letter in early March 1840, "I do not think my prospects individually are very flattering, for I think it is probable I shall not be permitted to be a candidate."[81] If that fate had befallen Lincoln he would have been devastated, realizing that the political foundation he had built and the esteem of colleagues and citizens he had worked so hard to foster stood in serious jeopardy.

Lincoln felt marginally better about his political chances on March 14, 1840. The Sangamon County Whigs held a party convention—a practice that Lincoln and the Whigs had rebuked the Democrats for just four years earlier. Convention delegates officially nominated Lincoln for another term as state representative. In a letter written shortly thereafter to Stuart, Lincoln cynically theorized that he received the nomination only because he was "necessary to make stump speeches."[82] But rather than wallow in self-pity, he vowed to remain positive and work energetically for the 1840 Whig ticket. Party leaders tapped him for the honor of serving as a Whig presidential elector for candidate William Henry Harrison, who was the former Indiana governor, U.S. senator, and hero of the Battle of Tippecanoe in the

War of 1812. This role emboldened Lincoln. The task would send him on a stumping tour throughout the state to affirm Whig principles and tout Harrison's accomplishments.[83] He remained a firm party man, dedicated to "sustaining of those great principles for which the Whig party are now contending."[84] He assisted in editing the *Old Soldier,* an 1840 Harrison campaign newspaper. As party leader he likely assisted in the funding of it as well.[85]

Wearing his partisan stripes proudly, Lincoln continued to contribute anonymous articles to the *Journal*—relaying dispatches about legislative activity while in session, and ribbing Democrats for their stances. While Lincoln wrote pseudonymously, his targets were familiar with his verbal style, and suspected him of writing the articles. In 1840, the *Register* referred to an attack article as the cowardly work of "one of the Junto, whose members deliberate in secret, write in secret, and work in darkness—men who dare not let the light of day in upon their acts."[86]

As with previous campaigns, Lincoln witnessed plenty of the rough-and-tumble game of politics in which a fistfight might break out at any moment. Lincoln continued to use his great physical strength as a political asset. While accompanying Edward Baker at an event in 1839, a noisy and hostile crowd physically threatened Baker. Lincoln leaped to the platform, waved a stone pitcher in the air, and threatened to whack the first person who touched Baker, shouting, "I am here to protect him, and no man shall take him from this stand if I can prevent it." It had the desired effect and the crowd calmed.[87]

As a Whig presidential elector in 1840, Lincoln offered stern defenses of the Whig party, which inevitably pitted him against the Democrats' chosen state leader Stephen Douglas. At one speaking event in 1839, Lincoln failed to deliver a powerful performance, a rarity for him. A few days later he begged event officials to be allowed to redeem himself, and that time he exceeded expectations. Fellow legislator and friend Joseph Gillespie joyfully recalled, "I never heard and never expect to hear such a triumphant vindication as he then gave of Whig measures or policy. He never after to my knowledge fell below himself."[88]

Lincoln continued to polish his oratorical skills, peppering his speeches with humorous anecdotes and stories that would resonate with his rural constituents. Robert Wilson marveled at Lincoln's "mode of reasoning," his "inexhaustible" memory for facts and anecdotes, and how he could apply those to the situation at hand.[89] An observer at an 1840 Whig rally noted that Lincoln "discussed the questions of the time in a logical way, but much time was devoted to telling stories to illustrate some phase of his argument, though more often the telling of these stories was resorted to for the purpose of rendering his opponents ridiculous."[90] At an event in Alton, a reporter captured the scene of a Lincoln speech, writing that his talk succeeded in being "highly argumentative and logical, enlivened by numerous anecdotes, [and was] received with unbounded applause."[91] Even Democratic reporters showered occasional praise on him, one writing that he "always replies jacosely and in good humor . . . and he is therefore hard to foil."[92]

That is not to say that everyone felt persuaded by Lincoln's urbanity. In Belleville in April 1840, the Democratic newspaper *Missouri Republican* wrote that Lincoln gave a "weak, puerile, and feeble" effort. "Poor Lincoln!" the paper exclaimed.[93] The *Register* called Lincoln "used up" and "rotten to the core." Nor did newspapers fail to describe Lincoln's lack of handsomeness. At a Whig rally in Carlinville in April 1840, where it is said he spoke with "power and elegance," the local Democratic paper referred to him as "the lion of the Tribe of Sangamon . . . and the judgement from outward appearance, originally from Liberia."[94]

While perfecting his public speaking Lincoln persisted in sharp verbal attacks against his opponents. Joseph Gillespie warmly recalled that Lincoln was "remarkably tender of the feelings of others and never wantonly offended even the most despicable," but conceded that he "was a man of great nerve when aroused."[95] Robert Wilson also admitted that Lincoln "preserved his temper," and "when provoked," "used the weapons of sarcasm and ridicule, and always prevailed."[96] At an 1840 meeting in Springfield, local Democratic leader Dick Taylor, a man of fine style, denounced the Whigs as wealthy aristocrats who exploited the common man. Lincoln immediately reacted by jumping to the stage, pulling at Taylor's vest to reveal him donning a ruffled shirt and a gold watch and chain. Lincoln was not reluctant to use his poverty if it pleased the crowd or to paint a political opponent as elitist.

He gleefully mocked that while Taylor "was riding in a carriage, wore his kid gloves and had a gold headed cane," he had been "a poor boy hired on a flat boat at eight dollars a month, and had only one pair of breeches and they were buckskin." To the delight of the crowd, Lincoln asked, "If you call this aristocracy, I plead guilty to the charge."[97]

Despite Gillespie's avowal that Lincoln never "wantonly offended," Lincoln's harsh words occasionally did border on hurtful. He had not yet learned how to temper his emotions in the heat of the moment. Even Lincoln later confessed, "I'm one of the thinnest skinned men to any marks of impatience."[98] His words in a speech in Lawrenceville were apparently antagonistic enough to rile Wayne County Democratic state representative William Anderson. Following a speech there, Anderson wrote to Lincoln stating, "I think you were the aggressor. Your words imported insult. Please inform me on this point and if you designed to offend me." Lincoln responded apologetically, "I entertain no unkind feeling to you, and none of any sort upon the subject, except a sincere regret that I permitted myself to get into such an altercation."[99]

None illustrates Lincoln's propensity to engage in unthinking and spontaneous actions in this time more than his "skinning" of Jesse Thomas. In a campaign speech in late 1840 local Democratic leader Jesse Thomas criticized the tactics of the Long Nine. Lincoln was not in attendance but friends immediately sent for him. He arrived just as Thomas concluded his speech. Lincoln marched to the stage to give a rebuttal. Since he had not heard the contents of Thomas's address, he instead scathingly mimicked Thomas's gestures, his walk, and his speaking abilities. Lincoln delivered a performance so exacting that it filled the audience with raucous laughter and reduced Thomas to tears. The *Register* condemned the "rude assault," declaring that "Mr. Lincoln . . . has fallen into the ditch which he dug for his neighbor."[100] William Herndon wrote that the incident was so unlike Lincoln.

Lincoln, too, felt he went too far in his invective, and admitted it "filled him with the deepest chagrin." He subsequently apologized to Thomas, and all parties soon forgot the incident.[101]

If at times the intensity of the moment fueled Lincoln to spontaneously react, he could also calmly come to the defense of those under attack. He demonstrated this with Usher Linder, who had been opposite Lincoln in several legislative floor debates. In late 1839 while Linder—now a Whig—delivered a rousing speech in the statehouse, several rowdy hooligans personally insulted Linder and threatened to harm him when he departed the building. Lincoln and Edward Baker, once Linder's political opponents, moved into action. Before Linder exited the stage, the pair positioned themselves on either side of him and escorted him out of the building. With Linder on his arm, Lincoln told him, "Your quarrel is our quarrel, and that of the great Whig party of this nation, and your speech upon this occasion is the greatest one that has been made by any of us, for which we wish to honor, love, and defend you."[102] Upon arriving safely to his hotel, supporters cheered and Linder beamed with pride. Linder noted that "this was one of the proudest days of my life; not so much on account of the applause paid me by the multitude, as on account of the devoted friendship shown by Lincoln and Baker."[103]

Lincoln erred and made mistakes along the way, as does anyone who strives to test the waters of ambition and success. Robert Wilson spent many hours with Lincoln, watching him and learning from him as a mentor, just as Lincoln had learned from Stuart. Wilson heaped generous praise upon Lincoln, remarking in 1840, "He seemed to be a born politician. We followed his lead; but he followed nobody's lead. It may almost be said that he did our thinking for us." Then, where Wilson frankly admitted that Lincoln at times exhibited a "car[e]less and negligent" manner, he equally said of his role model, "He inspired respect."[104]

Despite the recent legislative defeat of the internal improvements projects that he so zealously championed and with it doubts as to his re-election chances, something awakened in Lincoln in 1839 and 1840. His stature as a Harrison presidential elector, his visibility and attention as a statewide spokesman for Whig policy, and his leadership position in the state legislature instilled in him a certain consciousness. Perhaps a bright political future still awaited him. Orville Browning contended that at this time Lincoln realized that "he was born for better things than then seemed likely or even possible."[105] Herndon corroborated, writing that, by 1840, Lincoln "had begun to dream of destiny."[106]

A FINAL TERM AND A
FUTURE UNDETERMINED

From the moment he arrived in Springfield, Lincoln doubted his ability to fit in. But by 1839 and into 1840 his prominence in the state legislature and involvement in the town council gave him an entrée to parties and cotillions such as those at the home of his legislative colleague Ninian Edwards and his wife, Elizabeth. The fashionable Edwards home was among the finest in Springfield, complete with a lightning rod similar to the one Lincoln had teasingly chided Forquer for having.[1]

At the Edwards home Lincoln met many eligible bachelorettes, including Elizabeth's sister Mary Todd, who at the time lived with the Edwardses. Kentucky born, the twenty-year-old filled a room with her quick wit, lively and charming nature, knowledge of literature and foreign languages, and her attention to politics. Although Miss Todd could be quick-tempered, proud, and impulsive, many a Springfield bachelor vied for her attention. Stephen Douglas had escorted her to several balls and parties. Ten years older than Todd, Lincoln at first felt inadequate to compete for her affections, but he finally mustered the courage to ask her to dance. Although his dancing did nothing to charm her, she saw something quite likeable in him. The couple began a courtship, and by 1839 and into 1840 their contact became more frequent and their relationship deepened.[2]

Springfield State House. Lincoln and the Long Nine pushed to move the state capital to Springfield, which led to the building of this statehouse, where Lincoln served from 1839 to 1842. Courtesy of Library of Congress.

Miss Todd happened to be a cousin to John Stuart, which helped cement the budding alliance. Familiar with Lincoln's attributes and his flaws, Lincoln's law partner informed Todd about her suitor. Stuart relayed to her humorous stories of their times in the Black Hawk War. He boasted of Lincoln's quick study of politics and law, his towering intellect, his ability to apply lessons from the Bible and Shakespeare, and his marked ability to forcibly and eloquently express his thoughts. Stuart told Todd of Lincoln's scathing ridicule of political opponents, how his actions made audiences roar with laughter, and his effectiveness at converting the opposition to his side. She listened intently as Stuart complimented Lincoln's honesty, his unerring judgment, his ability to determine right from wrong, and his uncommon defense of the poor and helpless.[3]

Such accolades enticed Mary. She prided herself on her ability to judge men's motives and their potential to succeed. She surely sought a gentleman who could provide for her financially so that she might one day live in the type of comfort she had grown accustomed to from her wealthy Kentucky life. But she equally required a man with the potential to rise high up the political ladder. When asked whether she preferred Douglas or Lincoln, she purportedly answered, "The one that has the best chance of being president."[4] But Todd's cultivated and refined tastes presented a challenge for Lincoln's lack of wealth and formality. And by late 1840 his speaking tour for presidential candidate William Henry Harrison and the demands of the legal circuit left little time for Lincoln and Todd to spend together.

Lincoln's re-election prospects still weighed on him. Despite his doubts, on August 3, 1840, Lincoln and the Whig candidates captured all five available state legislative seats. In fact, Lincoln's popularity remained firm enough for him to take nearly six hundred votes more than the leading Democrat. But likely because of his ardent backing of the now-defunct internal improvements legislation and his role in mounting state debt, Lincoln had indeed lost support from the previous election—polling the lowest of all five winning candidates. The other four winners had never run before.[5]

In preparation for the November presidential election, Illinois Whigs came out in force to rally for William Henry Harrison. Despite the fact that Harrison had amassed substantive wealth, Whigs trumpeted Harrison's log-cabin roots and military heroism. To rally voters to their log-cabin and hard-cider campaign, Whigs held a massive three-day convention in Springfield. Lincoln most assuredly attended. Participants camped out, drank cider, ate barbeque, sang campaign songs, heard stirring speeches, listened to brass bands, and fired a canon. Whigs from Fayette County even brought in a real log cabin. An astounding twenty thousand people—nearly 5 percent of Illinois's total population—attended from all parts of the state. The crowd was so vast that one observer reckoned "the whole sucker state had broken loose."[6] Noted one critic of the spectacle: "It seemed as if pandemonium had been let loose on the earth."[7] Despite the invigorated Whig faithful in Illinois, Van Buren edged Harrison in the state's vote total while losing to him in the national election.

Soon afterwards, on November 23, 1840, the Twelfth General Assembly convened for a special session at the governor's beckoning specifically to address the interest on the accelerating state debt.

A regular session was slated to begin immediately following the adjournment of the special session. Whigs enjoyed a majority in the House briefly—for one term in 1838—but now it moved back to the Democrats, largely due to public worries over Whig support of internal improvements and mounting state debt. A total of 40 Whigs and 51 Democrats comprised the Illinois House; whereas the Senate had 14 Whigs and 26 Democrats. The statehouse was nearing completion, but could not yet be fully used. For the first few weeks of the special session the Senate met in their unfinished chamber of the new capitol building. The House of Representatives met in the unsuitable confines of the local Methodist church.[8]

The Whigs nominated Abraham Lincoln for House Speaker, and he received near unanimous party support. But it was not enough to upend the Democrats who, having the majority, voted to retain William Ewing in the position. Demonstrating Lincoln's popularity among his colleagues, he took the top party post as their floor leader for a third time. His interest in internal improvements earned him a spot on the Committee on Canals. He again resumed a seat on the Finance Committee.[9]

Among the freshman class of 1840 was Lyman Trumbull from St. Clair County. A man of intellect, at age sixteen the Connecticut-born Trumbull became a schoolteacher. Taking up law, he moved to Alton in 1837, where he established himself as a man of integrity, and voters elected him to the Illinois House in 1840. Trumbull had gained a reputation as difficult, but he and Lincoln formed a friendship and enjoyed mutual admiration. Though Trumbull had pledged himself to the Democrats, he recognized Lincoln's shrewd leadership in the legislature—who "stood in the front rank."[10]

Lincoln and the Whigs understood that Democrats would walk lockstep with the Van Buren administration's subtreasury idea and would support the federal mandate to pay only in gold and silver specie instead of paper money. The Bank of Illinois in Springfield had stopped paying in specie, and its charter lay in danger of being revoked. Very early in December 1840, during the special session that took place while the House was still meeting in the Methodist

Church, Whig leaders learned that the Democrats were planning to kill the state bank by exercising a law passed the previous year. The law mandated the bank in Springfield to resume specie payments at the conclusion of the "next ensuing session" of the General Assembly. So the Democrats plotted to end the current special session on December 5, and begin the regular session on December 7. Either the state banks would have to resume specie payments right then, or, even better, in the Democrats' minds, the state banks would fail to resume payment in specie and be forced to forfeit their charters and close. Hoping to forestall the end of the special session and the death of the state banks, the Whigs planned to outmaneuver the Democrats by preventing an adjournment of the special session—letting it run continuously into the regular session. This would give more time for the bank to operate through at least early March 1841.[11]

The Whigs' plan was simple: postpone the vote to adjourn the special session by not appearing. Without a quorum, no adjournment vote could take place, thus moving the House into a regularly scheduled session and saving the state banks. Several Whig members were convinced to stay away for much of the day of the vote to avoid a quorum. Other Whigs, including Lincoln, Joseph Gillespie, and Asahel Gridley of Bloomington watched merrily as Democrats scrambled to locate representatives. Democratic leaders summoned the House doorkeeper to go find absent legislators, but many he encountered declined to appear. Lincoln and his Whig colleagues, however, were unaware that several Democrats had snuck in, and Lincoln and his crew were unwittingly contributing to the attainment of a quorum. Once Lincoln realized this he sprang for the exit, but finding the door locked he hastily climbed out through a nearby window. Other Whigs followed but the trick failed.[12] The Democrats took the vote just in time and successfully adjourned the special session despite the "gymnastic performance of Mr. Lincoln and his flying brethren," as the *Illinois State Register* coined it.[13]

The press had a field day with the incident. The *Belleville Advocate* recorded that Lincoln "made an assault upon an unoffending window, through which he broke his way and made his escape, followed by two of his faithful adherents (Gillespie and Gridley) who slipped gracefully out of the window, and piled themselves beneath it upon the body of their chivalrous leader."[14] The *Register,* looking forward to the impending opening of the new capitol building, mocked Lincoln's foolish act and wrote that they would "inquire into the expediency of raising the State House one story higher, in order to have the House set in the third story so as to prevent members from jumping out of the windows. If such a resolution passes, Mr. Lincoln will in future have to climb down the spout."[15] Although Lincoln laughed off the episode, he regretted his actions. Weeks later in the new statehouse, Lincoln remarked that since the jumping scrape had become so celebrated it he should say something about it. His comment: from now on he would jump only when it pleased him to do so and no one should stop him.[16]

Leading efforts to kill the state banks, Lyman Trumbull moved to repeal the charter granting the bank its power as fiscal agent of the state, but his motion failed. Lincoln groused on the floor that he had grown "tired of this business" of the continual attempts to destroy the bank. He and Democratic representative John McClernand of Gallatin County engaged in a verbal tousle that grew exceedingly personal.[17] Days later Wickliff Kitchell of Montgomery County charged that the banks were "calculated to ruin the State."[18] Weary of the political nonsense, Democrat John Logan of Jackson County stepped in to provide a middle road and pointed to some of his fellow legislators as "total destructives" who "wished to destroy the canal, the Bank and everything." He portended that if the legislature dismantled the banks, the currency of the whole state would be cut off as well.[19] Logan's crucial support allowed the state banks to continue.

Of increased importance to the legislature was mounting state debt, largely the result of the Panic of 1837 and of the now-defunct internal improvements projects. Lincoln's membership in the Committee on Finance compelled him to act on finding options to alleviate the debt burden. Burdensome it was. By 1840 the state had accumulated a debt of over $14 million for a population of nearly five hundred thousand.[20] In early December 1840, Lincoln took to the podium in the House to propose that the governor be authorized to issue "Illinois Interest Bonds" to offset the accumulated interest on the state debt. Lincoln admitted he bore a "share of the responsibility devolving upon us in the present crisis"—an implicit apology for his relentless push for costly internal improvements projects. In the proposal, he also recommended a property tax at the rate of thirty cents for each hundred dollars of valued property. He guessed that these dual strategies might yield the state $12 million if there were individuals willing to purchase the bonds. Lincoln freely admitted he was no financier and that his proposals might not be long-term solutions, but he felt "satisfied" that they would adequately address the interest on the public debt.[21] The House took up Lincoln's interest bonds issue, and within days passed a bill authorizing $300,000 in bonds to be released, but they rejected the property tax.[22]

The interest bonds did lower the interest on the debt, but only for six months. In July 1841, the state defaulted on its interest payments. Meanwhile, interest charges on the state debt climbed to $800,000 annually.[23] By 1842, the state had collected roughly $98,500 on the bonds—a far cry from the projected $12 million. The *Sparta Democrat* captured the mood, bemoaning that "no state could be much worse than ours at present."[24]

By late December 1840, the House had moved into its new statehouse chambers. Members still upset over the capital relocation moved to ensure that the state collected the final installment—a $50,000 payment owed by the citizens of Springfield. But with the economic panic, raising that amount was difficult. The *Chicago Democrat* warned that if the citizens of Springfield could not come up with the money, they could lose the capital. On behalf of Springfield, the *Sangamo Journal* promised in reply, "We will fulfill our obligation."[25] Some legislators considered extending funds to relieve the city of its debt. Springfield resident Lincoln surprisingly disagreed. He appreciated "the kindly feelings that prompted the proposal," but insisted the city should hold up its end of the agreement.[26]

Then in mid-January 1841, halfway through the session, Lincoln suffered an emotional breakdown. He had long struggled with depression (or "hypo" as it was then termed), but that January he hit rock bottom. His depression emanated from his recent breakup with Mary Todd a few weeks prior. By late 1840, Lincoln and Todd had been courting for over a year. But over time he began to doubt their compatibility and questioned whether he could satisfy her emotional needs. Despite Lincoln's amiable nature, he outwardly failed to show Miss Todd much affection or warmth, and increasingly felt uncertain about the depth of his love for her. In Speed's words, Lincoln did not feel "entirely satisfied that his heart was going with his hand."[27] Lincoln decided to break their engagement via letter, similar to the course he had taken with Mary Owens. After discussing with Joshua Speed his situation and intent, Speed persuaded him to confront her personally. So sometime around January 1, 1841, he visited with Todd and asked her to release him. With reluctance and great sadness, she did so. He knew he had caused her pain, and he struggled with an indecisiveness over his own feelings that propelled him into a deep depression. The mood only compounded when Speed concurrently informed Lincoln that he planned to move back to Kentucky some-time after the first of the year. Melancholy gripped Lincoln intensely. Speed recorded that in this moment "a gloom came over him till his friends were alarmed for his life."[28]

For over a week in mid-January 1841 Lincoln dropped from the scene and did not participate in any legislative activity. One colleague wrote regarding the absence, "We have been very much distressed."[29] The despondent Lincoln turned to Springfield friend Dr. Anson Henry and boarded with him for the next week.[30] Lincoln relayed to Stuart at the time that Henry "is necessary to my existence."[31] When Lincoln did make a return to the legislature on January 19, according to a fellow representative he had been "reduced and emaci-ated in appearance and seems scarcely to possess strength enough to speak above a whisper." The legislator said of Lincoln that "his case at present is truly deplorable."[32] Not surprisingly, Lincoln's depres-sion became a topic of conversation. Lincoln admitted to Stuart, "I have, within the last few days, been making a most discreditable exhibition of myself in the way of hypochondriaism."[33] A few days later, Lincoln wrote again to Stuart revealing the depth of his depression: "I am now the most miserable man living. If what I feel were equally distributed to the whole human family, there would not be one cheerful face on the earth. Whether I shall ever be better I can not tell; I awfully forebode I shall not."[34]

But amid the enveloping depression, he felt a deep nudging within him. Speed recalled the heartfelt conversation: "He said to me that he had done nothing to make any human being remember that he had lived—and that to connect his name with the events transpiring in his day & generation and so impress himself upon them as to link his name with something that would redound to the interest of his fellow man was what he desired to live for."[35] That longing to make a difference in the world refueled Lincoln's drive, and gave him the will to press forward.

Only time, the help of friends, and immersion in his legislative duties gave Lincoln respite from his anguish. But slowly and eventually the deep gloom melted. A few weeks later Lincoln wrote to Stuart passing off his condition with the assurance that he was "neither dead nor quite crazy yet."[36] One incident in January suggests that Lincoln felt spirited enough to exercise his humor on the House floor. A debate ensued as to whether, based upon the 1840 Illinois census, the number of senators and representatives in the General Assembly should be reapportioned and increased. After Lincoln spoke against an increase, representative William Bissell of Monroe County jabbed Lincoln—now often called the "longest of the Long Nine"—saying that only old women were partial to the number nine. To that Lincoln stated, "If any woman, old or young, ever thought there was any peculiar charm in this distinguished specimen of number 9, I have, as yet, been so unfortunate as not to have discovered it." The quip was met with loud applause.[37] Incidentally, the final bill passed specifying that "each four thousand white inhabitants shall be entitled to one representative."[38]

Lincoln's moods were certainly not helped by the fate of the internal improvements projects. They had been largely killed in the previous session. Lyman Trumbull in November 1840 proposed to have the governor appoint an agency to assume control of the books and property of what remained of the dismantled internal improvements system. Lincoln opposed the move, mostly on grounds that such authority should remain in the hands of the legislature.[39]

In the face of mounting debt, the question arose as to the prudence of completing the Illinois and Michigan Canal or abandoning it. Lincoln voted with those wishing to push forward with its completion. In February 1841, Lincoln offered an amendment to the Illinois and Michigan Canal completion bill allowing the state to issue up to $3 million in bonds for all the necessary work to finish the project. Representative Wickliff Kitchell questioned the wisdom of such a move, reminding Lincoln that Illinois had already amassed a severe debt. Lincoln responded that completion of the canal would be a far more judicious and economical plan, and that if the work stopped it would swallow the state in even deeper debt and ruin. Kitchell then employed a Lincolnesque tactic by offering a humorous anecdote. He relayed that Lincoln reminded him of an Arkansas alcoholic who passed out stone drunk, and all attempts to revive him failed. His wife suggested brandy toddy as a remedy. As soon as the drunkard heard the words "brandy toddy," he shot up in bed and exclaimed, "That is the stuff." The only solution Lincoln could find for his ailment, Kitchell declared, was to "drink" more.[40]

Urged by his friendly colleagues to bring down Kitchell, Lincoln responded with an anecdote of his own. Kitchell reminded Lincoln of a hunter from Indiana who saw "big bugaboos" in everything. The man's brother caught him firing his gun at a tree one day, but couldn't determine what the target might be. Asking his brother what he was shooting at, the man replied it was a squirrel. The brother saw no squirrel but then noticed a louse crawling on the man's eyelashes. Lincoln concluded that the same problem plagued the gentleman from Montgomery: "He imagined he could see large squirrels every day, when they were nothing but lice."[41] The House erupted in raucous laughter. Despite attempts from the speaker to pound his gavel to regain control, men threw their hats, pounded their canes on the floor, and convulsed with laughter until tears were streaming down cheeks. Thanks in part to Lincoln's wit and savvy political persuasion, the bill for completion of the Illinois and Michigan Canal passed. It would be one of few enduring successes of the entire internal improvements system.[42]

Other actions of the legislature in the 1840–41 session included efforts to address funding in schools and efforts to improve the quality of teachers in Illinois. Lincoln voted aye on a resolution distributing school funding among counties proportionate to their population under age twenty. He also offered a resolution that the state set qualifications for individuals wishing to be teachers, maintaining that "no teacher shall receive any part of the public school fund who shall not have successfully passed such examination."[43] While the bill did not specify how to fund public education, these significant laws were in accord with the Northwest Ordinance of 1785 that every township in the state should have a section of land dedicated to building a school, and that those schools should have state-certified teachers. Lincoln's resolution would be incorporated into the common school code that remains today.[44]

In the Illinois race for U.S. senator, Democrat Samuel McRoberts become the first native Illinoisan elected to the U.S. Senate, defeating Cyrus Edwards and Edward Baker. McRoberts stood as a strong Jackson man, and it frustrated Lincoln that McRoberts had won only because of his patronage of the Democratic Party. "This affair of appointment to office is very annoying," Lincoln wrote to Stuart. "I am, as you know, opposed to removals to make places for our friends."[45] Of course, patronage appointments happened frequently, and had a Whig friend been elected, Lincoln would likely not have been so opposed.

In February 1841, Lincoln voted with the majority against the introduction of the secret ballot in Illinois.[46] It is odd to us today that publicly declaring one's choice in an election should be preferred over voting behind a curtain. However, the legislature reasoned that voting publicly and openly declaring one's choices encouraged, in governor Thomas Ford's words, "manly independence and frankness."[47]

Evidence of further partisan bickering, the Democratic-controlled House adopted a resolution aimed at William Henry Harrison. He had been elected president in November 1840 but had not yet been inaugurated. The resolution called for a one-term limit to be imposed on a president. Lincoln naturally voted nay in support of the Whig president. The term-limit resolution fell outside the purview of the state legislature's authority but passed regardless.[48] No second term was in store for Harrison anyway as he died after thirty-one days in office.

The legislature took up several bills that related to prisoners. Wickliffe Kitchell, who previously served as the state attorney general and was now back serving in the Illinois House, called for greater flexibility in prison sentences, including a provision abolishing the state death penalty. Judges commonly applied capital punishment for murder, but the death penalty could be applied to sundry other crimes including major theft, arson, and even perjury. Kitchell explained, "Life being given by God alone, it is believed that it ought not to be taken away by man, unless the safety of society most absolutely demands the sacrifice."[49] Lincoln voted in support of the measure, and the death penalty for a time met abolishment. The legislature, with Lincoln's support, approved another measure of abolishment: "that no smoking be allowed in the Hall during the hours of session."[50]

Mirroring the temperance movement permeating the nation, a few reform-minded legislators in this session introduced a measure prohibiting the sale of "vinous or spirituous liquors" within the state. If anyone would be caught selling such, he would face a draconian $1000 fine. Lincoln had no affinity for alcohol, but also saw no wisdom in its prohibition, and moved to table the motion. His motion failed, but the final vote among the hard-drinking ranks of the legislature killed the bill anyway, as only eight out of eighty-three voted for it.[51] Meanwhile, Lincoln supported a move to start daily session activity with prayer, which passed the House. However, the Senate apparently felt that they did not need to rely upon a higher power to guide their activities as they killed the measure.[52]

A growing concern met the legislature in 1841. A great number of Mormons fleeing religious persecution in Missouri flooded into the state beginning in 1839. They settled in western Illinois in the small community of Nauvoo. At first, Illinoisans extended sympathy to the Mormons. The *Sangamo Journal* in early 1841 called them "a persecuted people."[53] Much of the Nauvoo-area population, however, viewed the Mormons with suspicion and distrusted their religious practices and the political might they exercised. The religious group did not declare themselves either Whigs or Democrats, but both parties were conciliatory to them hoping to win their support. To provide assistance to the Mormons, Stephen Douglas—now Illinois secretary of state—orchestrated a move to have the legislature procure a charter for the Mormons to establish their own self-government. The charter would give unique powers to the community, allowing them to create their own legislature, court, and military. To appease the Mormons, a large majority of both Democrats and Whigs voted for the action, with Lincoln in concurrence. Several years later, however, the wide-scale authority granted to Mormons would come back to haunt the state when the religious group and the state clashed.[54]

The Mormons were not the only group both parties courted. Thousands of Irish workers came to work in America for the building of the canal, and Democrats encouraged them to vote for their party. A reading of the 1818 Illinois Constitution provided no clarity as to whether noncitizens were eligible to vote, but up to nine thousand foreign-born residents had joined the Democratic ranks with perhaps only a thousand supporting the Whigs. Fearing the political implications of those numbers, the Whigs charged the Democrats with fraud and decided to challenge the legality of noncitizens voting. They found a judge sympathetic to their cause: Dan Stone, the former Whig representative from Sangamon County.[55] Expecting an Illinois Supreme Court showdown, Democrats then sought to increase the number of high court judges on the bench from four to nine, and to have the state legislature—which they controlled—to appoint new judges. Stephen Douglas led the charge to draft a bill increasing the judiciary. Lincoln saw packing the court as an overtly partisan measure and appealed for an independent judiciary. He joined Senator Baker and thirty-three other Whigs in protest, saying that the Democrats plotted to reorganize the judiciary as purely "a party measure for party purposes," and argued that "it violates the great principles of the government by subjecting the Judiciary to the Legislature."[56] However, their protest was futile. The judicial increase measure passed the assembly, but if one Democrat would have switched sides it would have failed. In an apparent quid pro quo, the Democrats appointed Stephen Douglas to fill one of the new court vacancies. At age twenty-seven, he still holds the honor as the youngest-ever state supreme court justice.[57]

While it gained little notoriety at the time, the legislature also extended rights to another group. In a significant but little known initiative, Lyman Trumbull, in 1840, guided a bill through the legislature that allowed thirty-six hundred free blacks in Illinois to legally prove their freedom.[58] This was not to say that Illinois had become a safe haven for free blacks; just a few years earlier the General Assembly had debated a resolution prohibiting the migration of "negroes or mulattos" into the state.[59]

One of the final recorded votes of Abraham Lincoln as state representative was for the Cumberland Road—the nation's primary route from Maryland to Vandalia, Illinois—to be now extended to the western border of the state. To the end, Lincoln showed commitment to internal improvements, to expansion of the state, and as the bill read, to do "the wishes of the people of the State of Illinois."[60]

Lincoln felt relieved when the session ended in early March 1841. The January hypo and the increased committee work tested him severely, leading him to miss 92 of 397 roll call votes that session. He still received pay for the days when he took leave, and as usual for the Sundays in which no business transpired. He took his $392 with him and exited the doors of the capitol building for the last time as an active Illinois state representative.[61]

Lincoln strolled from the statehouse across the street to his law office. For now law would be his full-time occupation. Differences in politics and legal procedures separated Lincoln and law partner John Stuart, and though a friendship between the two remained, they dissolved their law partnership in early 1841. Lincoln joined as junior partner to Stephen T. Logan with whom he had already been working for several months.

The everyday matters of the law occupied Lincoln's mind and his time, but his political future was a different matter. He needed to weigh whether his legislative service still filled him with the same satisfaction it once had. His party would likely continue to remain in the minority in the legislature, so opportunities to rise further there were limited. He heard plenty of grumblings from voters upset over his undying devotion to the calamitous internal improvements system. The recent bout of melancholy also took a severe toll. Lincoln accepted that his tenure as state legislator had likely reached a sunset. "A change of scene might help me," he wrote to Stuart, ruminating on his state legislative service. A seat in Congress entered his mind as a possibility, but for now, Lincoln reflected, "If I could be myself, I would rather remain at home with Judge Logan."[62]

Friends and colleagues were not resigned to see Lincoln's political career come to a halt. Reflecting on Lincoln's status in 1841, a Springfield friend lamented, "I suppose he will now endeavor to drown his cares among the intricacies and perplexities of the law. No more will the merry peal of laughter ascend high in the air . . . as he succeeded in eliciting applause from some of the fair votaries by whom he was surrounded. . . . I fear his shrine will now be deserted and that he will withdraw himself from the society of us inferior mortals."[63]

Neither were newspapers fully ready to admit the possibility of Lincoln's departure from state politics. The *Fulton Telegraph* signaled in October 1841 their hope that Lincoln might be the Whig candidate for governor. The *Sangamo Journal* applauded that endorsement, writing, "The *Fulton Telegraph* pays just compliment to Mr. Lincoln." But the *Journal* sensed Lincoln's unwillingness to seek the office. The newspaper concluded, "His talents and services endear him to the Whig party but we do not believe he desires the nomination."[64]

During the summer of 1841, Lincoln decided to lift his spirits with a three-week trip to Farmington, Kentucky, to visit Joshua Speed, who had departed Springfield the previous January. Lincoln enjoyed his stay greatly, traveling and visiting with Speed and his fiancée, Fanny. He needed the respite to gain some perspective on his life.

Reconnection with the hills of his native state brought comfort and solace. Lincoln greatly missed the simplicity of life outside politics, and he missed the camaraderie of his friend Speed. "If we have no friends, we have no pleasure," he relayed to him.[65]

But however refreshing his excursion in the near South may have been, he returned to Springfield unmoved in his decision not to seek another term for the legislature. Whig contemporaries in the county who admired the accomplishments of their senior representative would have no talk of him stepping away. In March 1842 the *Register* reported that after "several recent meetings of the Springfield Junto" the candidates for the Illinois General Assembly would be William Butler, Ninian W. Edwards, John Dawson, and Lincoln." While Edward Baker and other Whig candidates strongly advocated Lincoln's candidacy, the *Register* predicted that "Mr. Lincoln, perhaps, will not accept the nomination."[66] The prediction proved correct, and he thenceforth made no overtures toward the seat.

Lincoln felt confident he left the Sangamon County delegation in good hands. He encouraged his law partner Stephen Logan to throw his hat in the ring for representative. "Our ticket is very popular— and will certainly succeed with great ease," Lincoln wrote to Speed.[67] He likewise cheered on his friends outside the county to return to the legislature. To Frederick Thomas from Lawrence County he teased, "Tell J. K. Dubois he must come to the Legislature again; that I am off the track, and that the wheels of government will inevitably stop with out the aid of one of us."[68] With that, the door on his legislative career closed.

What is to be made of the legacy that Lincoln as a state legislator left to Illinois? His accomplishments are notable. He had entered an unpopular protest against the evils of the institution of slavery. He pushed through internal improvements to advance the economic position of Illinois. He championed a state bank to create a system of available credit for those who had none. He muscled through the removal of the capital to a location more geographically centered in the state. He represented the wishes of the majority of his constituents especially in regard to county division and road requests. He participated in what would later be seen as landmark decisions by the state government concerning the Illinois and Michigan Canal, the incorporation of Chicago, and the establishment of public schools in the state. The initiatives passed by the Illinois General Assembly from 1834 to 1841, which Lincoln largely backed, envisioned Illinois as one of the leading states in the Union. In 1832 the state stood at the cusp of growth. A decade later, Illinois' agricultural output and emerging commercial industry rivaled any state west of the Appalachian Mountains. Settlers continued to pour in from the East and South, and from outside the country's borders. The state provided fertile soil for politicians too. Some of the nation's most prominent political names of the 1850s—Abraham Lincoln, Stephen Douglas, Orville Browning, and Lyman Trumbull among them—were all products of the Illinois state legislature of the 1830s and 1840s. And the character and integrity Lincoln displayed throughout his tenure left very few with anything negative to say about him.

But there were costs to progress. The state accumulated funding obligations out of proportion to its resources. Thanks in part to the costly internal improvements programs that Lincoln avidly promoted, by the time he left the state legislature, Illinois debt amounted to more than $15 million—an egregious amount for a budding state—a debt that Lincoln chose largely to ignore. The state would not completely pay off its debts until 1881. The prized internal improvements programs stopped cold, and the railroad tracks were temporarily abandoned. Only twenty-four miles of track lay complete when Lincoln exited the legislature. The Illinois and Michigan Canal got built only because Governor Thomas Ford, in 1845, persuaded private investors abroad to fund the completion of the project. The charters of the Bank of Illinois at Springfield and at Shawneetown were later eventually dissolved, ending the long and sordid saga of the state bank debate.[69]

Long after his career as state representative had passed, with the opportunity to look back on those years, Lincoln never retreated from the conviction that his advocacy for internal improvements had been right. To the end, Lincoln remained either resolute or stubborn, depending upon one's perspective. In his defense, his actions consistently reflected his beliefs. His promotion of internal improve-ments and of banks mirrored his philosophy of the right to rise for all and his conviction that it is the government's duty to provide an avenue for citizens to rise. Enduring intense pressure, Lincoln swore fidelity to that position and to that creed. As he said in a speech in 1839: "The probability that we may fall in the struggle *ought not* to deter us from the support of a cause we believe to be just; it *shall not* (his emphasis) deter me."[70]

Lincoln had attempted his first run for the legislature in 1832 as an unknown twenty-three-year-old. Departing from the statehouse in 1841 just shy of thirty-two he had achieved much. To be certain, he experienced many personal trials and stormy relationships. Ten years after his political career began he still showed little affinity for refinement and culture. At times he still exhibited more the actions of a shrewd partisan than a gifted statesman. He still tested the waters of his self-control and maturity, engaging in one final political attack against state auditor James Shields in 1842 before it nearly landed him in a duel. But in that eight years he gained far more than the $1,952 in total earnings for his four terms in the state legislature.[71] He had developed a thirst for public service, tested his political acu-men, cultivated an impressive oratorical style, practiced the art of compromise, tried his hand at political persuasion, given free rein to his inquisitiveness, and wrestled with his moral convictions. Above all, Lincoln had developed friends, and his thirst for distinction had earned him prominence and esteem, just as he had hoped from the outset. Just before Lincoln's term expired, Judge Stephen Douglas was asked what he thought of his formidable partisan opponent. Douglas admitted, "He is the ablest man in his party in the State, and a leader among men in everything he undertakes." Douglas declared that the man with whom he had often sparred had won "the respect and generally the confidence of every one."[72]

In 1842 Lincoln's colossal destiny remained unforeseen. Yet through his service in the Illinois legislature his true calling as a humble ser-vant of the people had unmistakably emerged. Ralph Waldo Emer-son, in his memorial to Lincoln, eloquently measured the eminence of this prairie legislator when he wrote, "A representative in the rural

Legislature of Illinois—on such modest foundations the broad structure of his fame was laid. How slowly, and yet by happily prepared
steps, he came to his place."[73]

Indeed, just eight years after he had sauntered into the sleepy town
of New Salem in 1831 as a friendless stranger, Lincoln leaped onto the
stage of state politics as a prominent politician, and placed himself
on a path that would lead him into the pages of history.

* * *

Desk used by Lincoln. This desk is believed to be the one Lincoln used as
a legislator in the statehouse in Springfield. Courtesy of Lincoln Heritage
Museum.

EPILOGUE

In 1842, following the near duel with James Shields, Lincoln took to a more settled life. He married Mary Todd in November of that year. As his state legislative career ended, Lincoln pondered a run for Congress. In 1843 he found himself opposed for the seat by John J. Hardin and Edward Baker, both of whom he had served with in the state legislature. He waited his turn while enjoying a flourishing law career, and after a one-term stint in Congress from 1847 to 1849, he returned to practicing law as senior partner with William Herndon. Lincoln was elected to the state legislature one final time in 1854 but declined to take the seat in order to continue his legal practice and focus on a possible bid for the U.S. Senate.

After the Kansas-Nebraska Act "reawakened" him to politics in 1854, the Whig-turned-Republican Lincoln faced the formidable Stephen Douglas in a race for the U.S. Senate in 1858. Although he lost, Lincoln's 1858 defeat positioned him as an 1860 presidential candidate.

Many of the same men whom Lincoln met and befriended in the Illinois state legislature became accomplished national politicians. Lyman Trumbull, Orville Browning, James Shields, and Stephen Douglas all enjoyed terms as U.S. senators from Illinois. Many of Lincoln's legislative colleagues remained personally and professionally close to him. Archibald Williams, William Fithian, and Jesse Dubois were instrumental in campaigning for Lincoln in 1858 and 1860. Several former legislative colleagues—John Stuart, Joseph

Gillespie, Robert Wilson, Edward Baker, Orville Browning, and Stephen Douglas, among others—visited Lincoln as friends in the White House, despite, in some cases, their differing political views. Many of the postlegislature encounters resulted in touching stories, such as in the case of the fiery Usher Linder, who often opposed Lincoln in the legislature. Linder's son Daniel joined the Confederacy and was captured and held in a Union prison, only to receive a merciful release from President Lincoln and be sent home to his grateful father.

Lincoln's presidential accomplishments are familiar to the reader, as is his dreadful fate at the hands of an assassin who ended his remarkable life. How poignant and symbolic that the final place where Lincoln's body lay in state before his interment in May 1865 would be the chamber of the Illinois House of Representatives in Springfield. There, his public life began. How appropriate that there he should be viewed one final time.

NOTES
INDEX

NOTES

Preface

1. Compiled in the *Journal of the House of Representatives of the State of Illinois* (9th–12th sessions), 1834–41.

1. Citizen Lincoln, Candidate Lincoln

1. Abraham Lincoln, "To Martin S. Morris," March 26, 1843, in *The Collected Works of Abraham Lincoln*, ed. Roy P. Basler (New Brunswick, NJ: Rutgers University Press, 1953) 1:320.

2. Roy P. Basler, ed., "James Quay Howard's Notes on Lincoln," *The Abraham Lincoln Quarterly* 4, no. 8 (December 1947): 396.

3. Benjamin P. Thomas, *Lincoln's New Salem* (Springfield: Abraham Lincoln Association, 1934), 45.

4. Thomas, *Lincoln's New Salem*, 24.

5. James Short to William H. Herndon, in *Herndon's Informants: Letters, Interviews, and Statements about Abraham Lincoln*, ed. Douglas L. Wilson and Rodney O. Davis (Urbana: University of Illinois Press, 1998), 73.

6. Abner Y. Ellis to WHH, in *Herndon's Informants*, 501. See also Benjamin P. Thomas, *Abraham Lincoln: A Biography* (New York: Modern Library, 1952), 42.

7. Paul E. Simon, *Lincoln's Preparation for Greatness: The Illinois Legislative Years* (Norman: University of Oklahoma Press, 1965), 4.

8. Jason Duncan to WHH, *Herndon's Informants*, 539.

9. Francis Fisher Browne, *The Every-Day Life of Abraham Lincoln* (New York: N. D. Thompson, 1886), 44.

10. William G. Greene to WHH, *Herndon's Informants*, 11.

11. William Baringer, *Lincoln's Vandalia: A Pioneer Portrait* (New Brunswick, NJ: Rutgers University Press, 1949), 7.

12. Thomas, *Abraham Lincoln*, 24.

13. Augustus Mitchell, *Illinois in 1837* (Philadelphia: Grigg and Elliot), 50.

14. Thomas, *Lincoln's New Salem*, 42.

15. Simon, *Lincoln's Preparation for Greatness*, 14.

16. N. W. Branson to WHH, *Herndon's Informants*, 91.

17. Allen C. Guelzo, *Abraham Lincoln: Redeemer President* (Grand Rapids, MI: Wm. B. Eerdmans Publishing, 1999), 48.

18. Robert B. Rutledge to WHH, *Herndon's Informants*, 385.

19. Ibid.

20. Ward Hill Lamon, *The Life of Abraham Lincoln* (Boston: James R. Osgood and Company, 1872), 121.

21. J. Rowan Herndon to WHH, *Herndon's Informants*, 6.
22. Lincoln, "Autobiography Written for John L. Scripps," c. June 1860, *CW* 4:64.
23. Thomas, *Lincoln's New Salem*, 49.
24. Lincoln, "Communication to the People of Sangamon County," March 9, 1832, *CW* 1:8.
25. Ibid., 9.
26. Ibid., 8–9.
27. Abner Y. Ellis to WHH, *Herndon's Informants*, 171.
28. Lincoln, March 9, 1832, *CW* 1:8.
29. Ibid.
30. Ibid.
31. Lincoln, March 9, 1832, *CW* 1:6.
32. Lincoln, March 9, 1832, *CW* 1:6–7. See also Ida Tarbell, *The Early Life of Abraham Lincoln* (New York: McClure, 1896), 125.
33. William H. Herndon and Jesse W. Weik, *Herndon's Life of Lincoln* (New York: Da Capo Press, 1942), 72.
34. Thomas Gaines Onstot, *Pioneers of Menard and Mason Counties* (Forest City, IL: T. G. Onstot, 1902), 40.
35. Lincoln, March 9, 1832, *CW* 1:7
36. Simon, *Lincoln's Preparation for Greatness*, 8.
37. Lincoln, "Speech in the Illinois Legislature concerning the State Bank," January 11, 1837, *CW* 1:64.
38. Lincoln, "Fragment on Government," April 1, 1854, *CW* 2:221.
39. For background on Lincoln's political philosophy see William Lee Miller, *Lincoln's Virtues* (New York: Alfred A. Knopf, 2007), 109–13; and Richard Carwardine, *Lincoln: A Life of Purpose and Power* (New York: Alfred A. Knopf, 2003), 14–15.
40. Lincoln, March 9, 1832, *CW* 1:8.
41. Robert V. Remini, *The Life of Andrew Jackson* (New York: HarperCollins, 2011), 307. A full biography of Jackson and his political influence in America can be found in Arthur M. Schlesinger Jr., *The Age of Jackson* (Boston: Little, Brown and Company, 1952).
42. A discussion of the effect of Henry Clay can be found in Clement Eaton, *Henry Clay and the Art of American Politics* (Boston: Little, Brown and Company, 1957).
43. Edgar DeWitt Jones, *The Influence of Henry Clay upon Abraham Lincoln* (Lexington, KY: Henry Clay Memorial Foundation, 1952), 17. See also Guelzo, *Abraham Lincoln*, 57–60.
44. Thomas, *Lincoln's New Salem*, 49.
45. Katharine L. Dvorak, "Peter Cartwright and Charisma," *Methodist History* 26, no. 2 (Jan. 1988): 113–26.

46. "Conversation with Hon. Wm. Butler," in Michael Burlingame, ed., *An Oral History of Abraham Lincoln: John G. Nicolay's Interviews and Essays* (Carbondale: Southern Illinois University Press, 1996), 20.

47. Ibid.

48. Lincoln, c. June 1860, *CW* 4:64. Further information in Thomas, *Lincoln's New Salem*, 57.

49. Thomas, *Lincoln's New Salem*, 57.

50. Onstot, *Pioneers*, 54.

51. Herndon and Weik, *Herndon's Lincoln*, 86.

52. J. Rowan Herndon to WHH, *Herndon's Informants*, 7.

53. "Conversation with Hon. J. T. Stuart," in Burlingame, *Oral History*, 10.

54. "Conversation with Hon. Wm. Butler," in Burlingame, *Oral History*, 15.

55. Onstot, *Pioneers*, 60.

56. "John G. Nicolay and John Hay," in *Lincoln Reader*, ed. Paul M. Angle (New Brunswick, NJ: Rutgers University Press, 1947), 47.

57. Thomas, *Lincoln's New Salem*, 58.

58. "Conversation with Hon. S. T. Logan," in Burlingame, *Oral History*, 35–36.

59. Jason Duncan to WHH, *Herndon's Informants*, 541–42.

60. Theodore Calvin Pease, *Illinois Election Returns, 1818–1848* (Springfield: Illinois State Historical Library, 1923), 262.

61. Lincoln, c. June 1860, *CW* 4:64.

62. Lamon, *Life of Abraham Lincoln*, 135.

2. A Prominent and Partisan Politician

1. Lincoln, "Autobiography Written for John L. Scripps," c. June 1860, *CW* 4:65.

2. Josiah Gilbert Holland, *Life of Abraham Lincoln* (Springfield, MA: Gurdon Bill, 1866), 55. See Deed Record J, 515, IRAD, University of Illinois Springfield.

3. Lincoln, c. June 1860, *CW* 4:64–65.

4. Thomas, *Lincoln's New Salem*, 69, 116–17.

5. Robert L. Wilson to WHH, *Herndon's Informants*, 201–2.

6. Ibid., 203.

7. Thomas, *Lincoln's New Salem*, 76.

8. Lamon, *Life of Abraham Lincoln*, 125.

9. Stephen Mansfield, *Lincoln's Battle with God* (Nashville: Thomas Nelson, 2012), 61–62.

10. Herndon and Weik, *Herndon's Lincoln*, 103.

11. Charles Maltby, *The Life and Public Services of Abraham Lincoln* (Stockton, CA: Daily Independent Print, 1884), 44, quoted in Burlingame, *Abraham Lincoln* (Baltimore: Johns Hopkins University Press, 2008), 82.

12. Joseph Gillespie to WHH, *Herndon's Informants*, 182.

13. Maltby, *Public Services*, 44.

14. J. Rowan Herndon to WHH, *Herndon's Informants*, 7–8.

15. Thomas, *Lincoln's New Salem*, 75–76.

16. "Conversation with Hon. S. T. Logan," in Burlingame, *Oral History*, 36.

17. J. Rowan Herndon to WHH, *Herndon's Informants*, 7–8.

18. Henry T. Rankin, *Personal Recollections of Abraham Lincoln* (New York: G. P. Putnam's Sons, 1916), 101–02; and Albert Beveridge in *Lincoln Reader*, 79.

19. Richard Lawrence Miller, *Lincoln and His World: Prairie Politician, 1834–1842* (Mechanicsburg, PA: Stackpole Books, 2008), 147.

20. "Conversation with Hon. J. T. Stuart," in Burlingame, *Oral History*, 10.

21. Thomas, *Lincoln's New Salem*, 75.

22. "Conversation with Hon. S. T. Logan," in Burlingame, *Oral History*, 36.

23. Thomas, *Lincoln's New Salem*, 75.

24. "Conversation with Hon. J. T. Stuart," in Burlingame, *Oral History*, 11–12.

25. Ibid.

26. Ibid.

27. Baringer, *Lincoln's Vandalia*, 27.

28. Lincoln, c. June 1860, *CW* 4:65.

29. William O. Stoddard, *The True Story of a Great Life* (New York: Fords, Howard, and Hulbert, 1885), 102.

30. Douglas L. Wilson, *Lincoln before Washington* (Urbana, IL: University of Illinois Press, 1997), 302.

31. Angle, *Lincoln Reader*, 68.

32. Baringer, *Lincoln's Vandalia*, 11–15.

33. Ibid., 76.

34. Ibid.

35. "Conversation with Hon. J. T. Stuart," in Burlingame, *Oral History*, 13.

36. Thomas, *Abraham Lincoln*, 46; and Baringer, *Lincoln's Vandalia*, 64.

37. *Vandalia Union*, December 28, 1916. See also Thomas Lowry, *Personal Reminiscences of Abraham Lincoln* (Minneapolis: self-published, 1910), 22–23. Lowry maintains that Owen Lovejoy relayed the quote to him in 1863.

38. Ibid., 46; and Baringer, *Lincoln's Vandalia*, 47.

39. Baringer, *Lincoln's Vandalia*, 48–49.

40. Gov. Thomas Ford, *History of Illinois* (Chicago: S. C. Griggs and Co., 1854), 286.

41. Ronald C. White, *A. Lincoln: A Biography* (New York: Random House, 2009), 62.

42. Albert Beveridge in *Lincoln Reader*, 79.

43. "Conversations with Hon. J. K. Dubois," in Burlingame, *Oral History*, 30.
44. Albert Beveridge in *Lincoln Reader*, 80.
45. Thomas, *Abraham Lincoln*, 47.
46. Tarbell, *Early Life*, 197.
47. Mitchell, *Illinois in 1837*, v.
48. Ibid., vi.
49. Ford, *History of Illinois*, 169.
50. George W. Smith, *A Student's History of Illinois*, 5th edition (Chicago: Hall and McCreary, 1921), 118.
51. Robert P. Howard, *Illinois: A History of the Prairie State* (Grand Rapids, MI: William B. Eerdmans Publishing Company, 1972), 197–98.
52. Herndon and Weik, *Herndon's Lincoln*, 131.
53. Baringer, *Lincoln's Vandalia*, 51–52.
54. Simon, *Lincoln's Preparation for Greatness*, 26.
55. Lincoln, "Bill to Limit Jurisdiction of Justices of Peace," December 5, 1834, *CW* 1:26.
56. Simon, *Lincoln's Preparation for Greatness*, 26. See also Miller, *Lincoln and His World*, 24.
57. Lincoln, "Bill to Authorize Samuel Musick to Build a Toll Bridge," December 9, 1834, *CW* 1:28.
58. State of Illinois, *Journal of the House of Representatives of the Ninth General Assembly, First Session* (Vandalia: William Walters, 1836), 240, 245.
59. Harry E. Pratt, "Lincoln in the Legislature," Annual Meeting of the Lincoln Fellowship of Wisconsin, February 12, 1946.
60. Burlingame, *Abraham Lincoln*, 94. See also David Herbert Donald, *Lincoln* (London: Jonathan Cape, 1995), 59, for discussion on legislative business.
61. Herndon and Weik, *Herndon's Lincoln*, 130.
62. Paul E. Stroble Jr., *High on the Okaw's Western Bank, Vandalia, Illinois 1819–1839* (Urbana: University of Illinois Press, 1992), 49.
63. Mary Burtschi, *Vandalia: Wilderness Capital of Lincoln's Land* (Vandalia, IL: Little Brick House, 1977), 42–43.
64. Miller, *Lincoln and His World*, 147.
65. Thomas, *Abraham Lincoln*, 45.
66. Baringer, *Lincoln's Vandalia*, 62.
67. Wilson, *Honor's Voice*, 153–54.
68. John T. Stuart to WHH, *Herndon's Informants*, 481.
69. John T. Stuart to WHH, *Herndon's Informants*, 12–13.
70. For background on the canal, see Edward Ranney and Emily Harris, *Prairie Passage: The Illinois and Michigan Canal Corridor* (Urbana, IL: University of Illinois Press, 1998).
71. Ford, *History of Illinois*, 166, 179.

72. Miller, *Lincoln and His World*, 15.

73. Donald, *Lincoln*, 59.

74. Francis Fisher Browne, *The Everyday Life of Abraham Lincoln* (Chicago: Browne and Howell Company, 1914), 49.

75. *Sangamo Journal*, January 16, 1836.

76. For more information on the history of the bank, see Robert Remini, *Andrew Jackson and the Bank War: A Study in the Growth of Presidential Power* (New York: Norton Publishing, 1967).

77. The Lincoln Log, January 5, 1835, www.thelincolnlog.org.

78. *Journal of the House of Representatives of the Ninth General Assembly*, 1:258–59.

79. Ibid., 260–63. See also Thomas, *Abraham Lincoln*, 48; and Carwardine, *Lincoln*, 16–17.

80. Carl Sandburg, *Abraham Lincoln: The Prairie Years* (New York: Harcourt, Brace, and Company, 1926), 1:245.

81. "Report and Resolutions in Relation to Purchase of Public Lands," *CW* 1:135–38.

82. The Lincoln Log, January 10, 1835.

83. Thomas, *Abraham Lincoln*, 47.

84. "The Life and Services of Joseph Duncan, Governor of Illinois, 1834–1838" in *Transactions of the Illinois State Historical Society* (Northern Illinois University, 1919), 119.

85. Simon, *Lincoln's Preparation for Greatness*, 30.

86. Lincoln, "Speech in Illinois Legislature concerning the Surveyor of Schuyler County," *CW* 1:31.

87. Baringer, *Lincoln's Vandalia*, 56.

88. "Conversations with Hon. J. K. Dubois," in Burlingame, *Oral History*, 31.

89. Simon, *Lincoln's Preparation for Greatness*, 22.

90. White, *A. Lincoln*, 64.

91. Herndon and Weik, *Herndon's Lincoln*, 133.

92. Abner Ellis to WHH, *Herndon's Informants*, 501.

3. Lawyer, Legislator, Logroller, Leader

1. Harry E. Pratt, *Personal Finances of Abraham Lincoln* (Springfield, IL: Abraham Lincoln Association, 1943), 22.

2. Isaac Cogdal to WWH, *Herndon's Informants*, 440.

3. The Lincoln Log, December 8, 1835.

4. Howard, *Illinois: A History of the Prairie State*, 211.

5. *Journal of the House of Representatives of the Ninth General Assembly* 2:27.

6. The Lincoln Log, January 5, 1836.

7. *Journal of the House of Representatives of the Ninth General Assembly* 2:44, 63.
8. Orlando B. Ficklin to WHH, *Herndon's Informants*, 58.
9. *Journal of the House of Representatives of the Ninth General Assembly* 2:8–12.
10. Lincoln, "To Thomas J. Nance," December 10, 1835, *CW* 1:38.
11. Thomas, *Abraham Lincoln*, 52.
12. Baringer, *Lincoln's Vandalia*, 68.
13. Thomas, *Abraham Lincoln*, 52. See also The Lincoln Log, January 11, 1836.
14. The Lincoln Log, February 27, 1836.
15. Lincoln, "Report to Illinois Legislature on State Expenses," January 2, 1836, *CW* 1:45.
16. Lincoln, "Resolution Introduced in Illinois Legislature . . . to Inquire into the Publishing of State Laws," December 28, 1835, *CW* 1:44.
17. 1830 and 1835 U.S. Census Bureau reports.
18. Simon, *Lincoln's Preparation for Greatness*, 21.
19. *Journal of the House of Representatives of the Ninth General Assembly* 2:107.
20. *Sangamo Journal*, July 2, 1836.
21. Browne, *Everyday Life of Abraham Lincoln*, 66.
22. Burlingame, *Abraham Lincoln*, 137.
23. *Sangamo Journal*, January 9, 1836.
24. *Journal of the House of Representatives of the Ninth General Assembly* 2:338–40.
25. The Lincoln Log, January 14, 1836.
26. Simon, *Lincoln's Preparation for Greatness*, 41.
27. The Lincoln Log, May 30, 1836.
28. Ibid., March 19, 1836.
29. Baringer, *Lincoln's Vandalia*, 45–46.
30. Lincoln, "To the Editor of the *Sangamo Journal*," June 13, 1836, *CW* 1:48.
31. Ibid.
32. Miller, *Prairie Politician*, 53.
33. June 13, 1836, *CW* 1:48.
34. Ibid.
35. Sandburg, *Prairie Years*, 191.
36. Lincoln, "To Robert Allen," June 21, 1836, *CW* 1:49.
37. Browne, *Everyday Life of Abraham Lincoln*, 57.
38. Herndon and Weik, *Herndon's Lincoln*, 137.
39. See Alexis de Tocqueville, *Democracy in America* (Chicago: University of Chicago Press, 2012).

40. Abraham Lincoln Association, Bulletin 36, no. 1, 7.
41. The Lincoln Log, July 11, 1836.
42. *Sangamo Journal*, July 16, 1836.
43. The Lincoln Log, July 17, 1836.
44. Lincoln, "Eulogy on Henry Clay," July 6, 1852, *CW* 2:126.
45. Robert L. Wilson to WHH, *Herndon's Informants*, 203; The Lincoln Log, July 30, 1836.
46. Herbert Mitgang, ed., *Lincoln as They Saw Him* (New York: Rinehart and Company Inc., 1956), 10–11.
47. Robert L. Wilson to WHH, *Herndon's Informants*, 202.
48. John Locke Scripps, *The First Published Life of Abraham Lincoln* (Cambridge, MA: Cranbrook Press, 1900), 40.
49. Pease, *Illinois Election*, 299.
50. Donald, *Lincoln*, 60.
51. Thomas, *Abraham Lincoln*, 56.
52. Albert Beveridge, in *Lincoln Reader*, 79.
53. "Conversations with J. K. Dubois," in Burlingame, *Oral History*, 30.
54. Baringer, *Lincoln's Vandalia*, 80.
55. *North Western Gazette and Galena Advertiser*, August 5, 1837.
56. *Sangamo Journal*, January 6, 1837.
57. Simon, *Lincoln's Preparation for Greatness*, 49.
58. Albert Beveridge, *Lincoln Reader*, 80.
59. Ibid.
60. Ibid.
61. White, *A. Lincoln*, 113–15.
62. Albert Beveridge, *Lincoln Reader*, 80.
63. Ibid.
64. Usher Linder, *Reminiscences of the Early Bar and Bench of Illinois* (Chicago: Chicago Legal News Company, 1879), 66.
65. Theodore Calvin Pease, ed., *Diary of Orville Hickman Browning* (Springfield: Illinois State Historical Library, 1927), xii.
66. Ibid.
67. Orville H. Browning to Isaac Arnold, in Burlingame, *Oral History*, 130.
68. Isaac N. Arnold, *Life of Abraham Lincoln* (Chicago: Jansen, McClurg, and Company, 1885), 50. See also Baringer, *Lincoln's Vandalia*, 83–84.
69. Thomas, *Abraham Lincoln*, 55.
70. Ibid., 58.
71. Harold Holzer, *Lincoln as I Knew Him* (Chapel Hill, NC: Algonquin Books, 2009), 37–38; Joseph Gillespie to WHH, *Herndon's Informants*, 180.
72. Lincoln, "To Mary S. Owens," December 13 1836, *CW* 1:54–55.
73. Thomas, *Abraham Lincoln*, 56.

74. Simon, *Lincoln's Preparation for Greatness*, 18.

75. Thomas, *Abraham Lincoln*, 56.

76. *Journal of the House of Representatives of the Tenth General Assembly* 1:18.

77. December 13, 1836, *CW* 1:54–55.

78. Elizabeth Duncan Putnam, "The Life and Services of Joseph Duncan," *Journal of the Illinois State Historical Society* 21, no. 1, April 1928.

79. December 13, 1836, *CW* 1:54–55.

80. The Lincoln Log, December 23, 1836.

81. *Journal of the House of Representatives of the Tenth General Assembly* 1:15–26.

82. Sandburg, *Prairie Years*, 193–4.

83. *Journal of the House of Representatives of the Tenth General Assembly*, 1:15–17.

84. Ibid.

85. Mitchell, *Illinois in 1837*, 58.

86. Baringer, *Lincoln's Vandalia*, 75. See also The Lincoln Log, November 19, 1836.

87. *Sangamo Journal*, November 26 and December 3, 1836.

88. William Herndon, *Lincoln Reader*, 83.

89. *Sangamo Journal*, November 26, 1836.

90. "Autobiography of Stephen Douglas," *Journal of the Illinois State Historical Society* 5, October 1912, 341.

91. Donald, *Lincoln*, 61.

92. Pease, *The Frontier State, 1818–1848* (Urbana: University of Illinois Press, 1987), 212–14.

93. *Journal of the House of Representatives of the Tenth General Assembly* 1:168–74.

94. Howard, *Prairie State*, 199–200.

95. Robert Sutton, "Illinois' Year of Decision, 1837," *Journal of the Illinois State Historical Society* 58 (April 1965), 36.

96. Pease, *Frontier State*, 211.

97. *Journal of the House of Representatives of the Tenth General Assembly* 1:53–55; see also Baringer, *Lincoln's Vandalia*, 93.

98. Miller, *Prairie Politician*, 114.

99. Howard, *Prairie State*, 198.

100. Thomas, *Lincoln's New Salem*, 87.

101. See Donald, *Lincoln*, 62; and Simon, *Lincoln's Preparation for Greatness*, 76–83. Both Donald and Simon refute that the Long Nine traded internal improvements votes for capital relocation votes, based on the fact that not all legislators who voted for the internal improvements bill voted likewise for the capital relocation bill. Indeed, a perfect quid pro quo may not have occurred. But, as I relay in this and later chapters,

the statements of many of Lincoln's colleagues—including some of the
Long Nine—make evident that the Long Nine put immense pressure
on the legislature to vote for both bills.

102. Burlingame, *Abraham Lincoln*, 116.
103. *Sangamo Journal*, April 22, 1837.
104. Miller, *Prairie Politician*, 133.
105. Herndon and Weik, *Herndon's Lincoln*, 139.
106. Burlingame, *Abraham Lincoln*, 119. *Sangamo Journal*, May 20, 1837.
107. *Illinois State Register*, July 20, 1838.
108. Ford, *History of Illinois*, 187.
109. Ibid.
110. Ibid.
111. Herndon and Weik, *Herndon's Lincoln*, 138.
112. Burlingame, *Abraham Lincoln*, 119.
113. "Conversation with Hon. S. T. Logan," in Burlingame, *Oral History*, 36–37.
114. Lamon, *Life of Abraham Lincoln*, 201.
115. "Conversations with Hon. J. K. Dubois," in Burlingame, *Oral History*, 30.
116. Ibid., 31.
117. As told by T. H. Henderson in *The Life of Abraham Lincoln* by Ida Tarbell (New York: McClure, 1900), 139.
118. Joshua F. Speed to WHH, *Herndon's Informants*, 499.
119. Wayne Whipple, *The Story-Life of Lincoln* (Philadelphia: John Winston Company, 1908), 137.
120. Thomas, *Abraham Lincoln*, 63.
121. "Conversation with P. Van Bergen," in Burlingame, *Oral History*, 34.
122. "Conversation with Hon. S. T. Logan," in Burlingame, *Oral History*, 37.
123. Herndon and Weik, *Herndon's Lincoln*, 175.
124. The Lincoln Log, December 23 and 24, 1836, and February 22, 1837.
125. *Journal of the House of Representatives of the Tenth General Assembly* 1:376–7 and 1:414.
126. *Journal of the House of Representatives of the Tenth General Assembly* 1:414.
127. Thomas, *Abraham Lincoln*, 60.
128. Donald, *Lincoln*, 62.
129. *Sangamo Journal*, June 16, 1838.
130. The Lincoln Log, December 20 and 21, 1836.
131. Baringer, *Lincoln's Vandalia*, 95–96.
132. The Lincoln Log, February 13, 1837.
133. Baringer, *Lincoln's Vandalia*, 97.

134. *Journal of the House of Representatives of the Tenth General Assembly* 1:414; The Lincoln Log, January 25, 1837.

4. Winning Legislation, Winning Esteem

1. Lincoln, "Speech in the Illinois Legislature concerning the State Bank," January 11, 1837, *CW* 1:64.
2. *Sangamo Journal*, January 28, 1837.
3. The Lincoln Log, January 18–19, 1837.
4. Thomas, *Abraham Lincoln*, 57–58.
5. White, *A. Lincoln*, 73.
6. Lincoln, "To Mary S. Owens," December 13, 1836, *CW* 1:54.
7. "Report to Illinois Legislature on Amount of Annual Revenue and Current Expenses," February 16, 1837, *CW* 1:74.
8. Thomas, *Abraham Lincoln*, 61–62.
9. Herndon and Weik, *Herndon's Lincoln*, 174.
10. Simon, *Lincoln's Preparation for Greatness*, 50.
11. Burlingame, *Abraham Lincoln*, 119.
12. *Journal of the House of Representatives of the Tenth General Assembly* 1:203.
13. The Lincoln Log, March 2, 1837.
14. *Journal of the House of Representatives of the Tenth General Assembly* 1:309–11; See also Baringer, 100.
15. *Journal of the House of Representatives of the Tenth General Assembly* 1:724–5.
16. *Illinois State Register*, March 6, 1837.
17. Ibid.
18. Mitchell, *Illinois in 1837*, v–vi.
19. *Journal of the House of Representatives of the Tenth General Assembly* 1:480.
20. Lincoln, "Amendments Introduced . . . Permanently Locating the Seat of Government of the State of Illinois," February 14, 1837, *CW* 1:73, note 1.
21. *Journal of the House of Representatives of the Tenth General Assembly* 1:592–94; see also Baringer, 105.
22. *Journal of the House of Representatives of the Tenth General Assembly* 1:752–9.
23. "Conversations with J. K. Dubois," in Burlingame, *Oral History*, 30.
24. Burlingame, *Abraham Lincoln*, 118.
25. *Journal of the House of Representatives of the Tenth General Assembly* 1:702.
26. Ibid., 752–9.
27. Ford, *History of Illinois*, 187.
28. Baringer, *Lincoln's Vandalia*, 110.

29. Donald, *Lincoln*, 64.
30. Ibid.
31. Thomas, *Abraham Lincoln*, 59.
32. Baringer, *Lincoln's Vandalia*, 98.
33. *Journal of the House of Representatives of the Tenth General Assembly* 1:669.
34. Baringer, *Lincoln's Vandalia*, 117.
35. *Journal of the House of Representatives of the Tenth General Assembly*, 1:667.
36. Lamon, *Life of Abraham Lincoln*, 209.
37. *Journal of the House of Representatives of the Tenth General Assembly* 1:242.
38. The Lincoln Log, January 20, 1837.
39. *Journal of the House of Representatives of the Tenth General Assembly* 1:309–11.
40. Lincoln, "Protest in Illinois Legislature on Slavery," March 3, 1837, *CW* 1:74–75.
41. Circa June 1860, *CW* 4:65.
42. "Speech in the Illinois State Legislature concerning the State Bank," January 11, 1837, *CW* 1:66.
43. Ibid.
44. Pratt, *Personal Finances*, 22.
45. William Butler to WHH, *Herndon's Informants*, 22.
46. Joshua F. Speed to WHH, *Herndon's Informants*, 589–90. See also Bryan S. Bush, *Lincoln and the Speeds: The Untold Story of a Devoted and Enduring Friendship* (Morley, MO: Acclaim Press, 2008).
47. Paul M. Angle, *Here Have I Lived* (Springfield: Abraham Lincoln Association, 1935), 90–92.
48. Burlingame, *Abraham Lincoln*, 129.
49. Burlingame, *At Lincoln's Side: John Hay's Civil War Correspondence and Selected Writings* (Carbondale: Southern Illinois University Press, 2000), 68.
50. Onstot, *Pioneers*, 34.
51. Angle, *Here Have I Lived*, 84–85.
52. *Mitchell, Illinois in 1837*, vi.
53. Lincoln, "To Mary S. Owens," May 7, 1837, *CW* 1:78.
54. Burlingame, *Abraham Lincoln*, 89.
55. Lincoln, "To Mary S. Owens," *CW* 1:78.
56. Thomas, *Abraham Lincoln*, 86.
57. Angle, *Here Have I Lived*, 71.
58. For background information, see: Ronald E. Seavoy, *An Economic History of the United States* (New York: Taylor and Francis Group, 2006).

59. *Journal of the House of Representatives of the Tenth General Assembly* 2:132–33.

60. Ibid.

61. Miller, *Prairie Politician*, 166.

62. Ibid., 170.

63. *Journal of the House of Representatives of the Tenth General Assembly* 2:132–33.

64. Ford, *History of Illinois*, 192.

65. White, *A. Lincoln*, 82.

66. Lincoln, "Bill Introduced in Illinois Legislature to Extend Corporate Powers," July 12, 1837, *CW* 81–82.

67. *Illinois State Register*, May 6 and June 17, 1837.

68. Walter B. Stevens, *A Reporter's Lincoln* (St. Louis: Missouri Historical Society, 1916), 8.

69. The Lincoln Log, August 3, 1837.

70. The Lincoln Log, July 25, 1837

71. Ibid.

72. Lincoln, "A Toast Volunteered at a Public Dinner at Springfield, Illinois," July 25, 1837, *CW* 1:87.

73. Thomas, *Abraham Lincoln*, 68. See also Donald, *Lincoln*, 74.

74. Thomas, *Abraham Lincoln*, 69.

75. Wayne C. Temple, "James Adams and Abraham Lincoln," *Illinois Lodge of Research* 16 (September 2007), 11.

76. Lincoln, "To Mary Owens," August 16, 1837, *CW* 1:94–95.

77. Thomas, *Abraham Lincoln*, 71.

78. See Joseph C. and Owen Lovejoy, *Memoir of the Rev. Elijah P. Lovejoy* (New York: John S. Taylor, 1838).

79. Angle, *Here Have I Lived*. See also Miller, *Prairie Politician*, 130.

80. Lincoln, "Address before the Young Men's Lyceum of Springfield, Illinois," January 27, 1838, *CW* 1:108–15. For a fuller discussion of the Lyceum address see Miller, *Prairie Politician*, 134–46.

81. Ibid.

82. Full discussion in George M. Fredrickson, "The Search for Order and Community," in *Public and Private Lincoln: Contemporary Perspectives*, ed. by Cullom David et al. (Carbondale: Southern Illinois University Press, 1979), 87–89.

83. Lincoln, Address before the Young Men's Lyceum," *CW* 1:108–15.

84. Rufus Rockwell Wilson, *Lincoln among His Friends: A Sheaf of Intimate Memories* (Caldwell, Idaho: Caxton Printers, 1942), 62.

85. Lamon, *Life of Abraham Lincoln*, 237.

86. Wilson, *Lincoln among His Friends*, 78.

87. Ibid., 480–81.

88. Ibid., 482.
89. January 27, 1838, *CW* 1:115.
90. Herndon and Weik, *Herndon's Lincoln*, 126.

5. The Prize and Price of Politics

1. *Sangamo Journal*, February 24, 1838.
2. Lincoln, "To William A. Minshall," December 7, 1837, *CW* 1:107.
3. Thomas, *Abraham Lincoln*, 73. See also Miller, *Prairie Politician*, 246.
4. Thomas, *Abraham Lincoln*, 73.
5. Browne, *Every Day Life of Abraham Lincoln*, 62.
6. The Lincoln Log, August 6, 1838.
7. Pease, *Illinois Election Returns*, 321.
8. Miller, *Prairie Politician*, 255.
9. Baringer, *Lincoln's Vandalia*, 116. See also The Lincoln Log, December 3, 1838.
10. Thomas, *Abraham Lincoln*, 73.
11. *Journal of the House of Representatives of the Eleventh General Assembly* 1:26–30. See also Miller, *Lincoln and His World*, 354.
12. *Journal of the House of Representatives of the Eleventh General Assembly* 1:26–30.
13. Miller, *Prairie Politician*, 354. See also The Lincoln Log, December 13, 1838.
14. *Sangamo Journal*, November 21, 1839.
15. Lincoln, "Discussion in Illinois Legislature . . . on Sub-Treasury," February 9, 1839, *CW* 1:135.
16. *Illinois State Register*, Jan. 8, 1840.
17. Lincoln, "Discussion in Illinois Legislature . . . on Sub-Treasury," February 9, 1839, *CW* 1:135.
18. Thomas, *Abraham Lincoln*, 74.
19. Lincoln, "Statement in Illinois Legislature concerning Internal Improvements," February 15, 1839, *CW* 1:144.
20. *Illinois State Register*, April 5, 1839.
21. Pease, *Frontier State*, 220.
22. The Lincoln Log, February 26, 1839; March 1, 1839.
23. D. W. Lusk, *Fifty Years of Illinois Politics and Politicians, 1809–1889* (Springfield, IL: H. W. Rokker, 1889), 79.
24. Lincoln, "Remarks in Illinois Legislature concerning . . . Purchase of Public Lands," January 17, 1839, *CW* 1:136.
25. Ibid.
26. Lincoln, "To William S. Wait," March 2, 1839, *CW* 1:147–8.
27. *Chicago Democrat*, May 22, 1839.
28. Baringer, *Lincoln's Vandalia*, 113.

29. *Sangamo Journal*, July 14, 1838.

30. Linder, *Reminiscences*, 62.

31. Ibid., 62–63.

32. Ibid., 63–64.

33. Lincoln, "To John T. Stuart," February 14, 1839, *CW* 1:143.

34. *Journal of the House of Representatives of the Eleventh General Assembly* 1:181–204. See also The Lincoln Log, January 9, 10, 11, 1839.

35. Paul J. Beaver, *Abraham Lincoln in Logan County* (Lincoln, IL: self-published, 2010), 76.

36. The Lincoln Log, February 6, 19, and 20. See also *Journal of the House of Representatives of the Eleventh General Assembly* 1:589–591.

37. Lincoln, "To William Butler," January 26, 1839, CW 1:139.

38. Lincoln, "Letter Written for Edward D. Baker to William Butler," January 26, 1839, *CW* 1:138.

39. Lincoln, "To William Butler," January 26, 1839, *CW* 1:139.

40. Lincoln, "To William Butler," February 1, 1839, *CW* 1:142.

41. The Lincoln Log, January 8, 1839.

42. Ibid., February 27, 1839.

43. See Seavoy. *An Economic History*, 127.

44. *Journal of the House of Representatives of the Eleventh General Assembly* 1:258.

45. Speech at Springfield, Illinois, December 18, 1839, *CW* 1:158.

46. Lincoln, "To William Butler," January 31, 1839, *CW* 1:140–41.

47. *Journal of the House of Representatives of the Eleventh General Assembly* 1:305–06. See also The Lincoln Log, January 24 and 29, 1839.

48. Lincoln, "Remarks in Illinois Legislature concerning . . . Fugitive Slaves," January 5, 1839, *CW* 1:126.

49. *Journal of the House of Representatives of the Eleventh General Assembly* 1:319.

50. Ibid., 1:371–2.

51. Ibid., 1:327, 391.

52. *Journal of the House of Representatives of the Eleventh General Assembly* 1:133.

53. Burlingame, *Abraham Lincoln*, 143.

54. Ibid., 146.

55. Pratt, *Personal*, 144.

56. Thomas, *Abraham Lincoln*, 75–77.

57. Lincoln, "Notice of a Public Meeting to Discuss the Revenue Law," April 5, 1839, *CW* 1:149.

58. Thomas, *Abraham Lincoln*, 75.

59. Herndon and Weik, *Herndon's Lincoln*, 151.

60. Lincoln, "Speech on the Subtreasury," December 26, 1839, *CW* 1:178.

61. Ibid., 1:172–73.
62. "Lincoln to John T. Stuart," January 20, 1840, *CW* 1:184.
63. *Sangamo Journal*, November 8 and December 5, 1839.
64. *Illinois State Register*, November 16, 1839.
65. *Illinois State Register*, November 23, 1839.
66. The Lincoln Log, January 24, 1840.
67. *Journal of the House of Representatives of the Eleventh General Assembly* 2:16–18.
68. Lincoln, "To John T. Stuart," January 20, 1840, *CW* 1:184.
69. Sandburg, *Prairie Years*, 242.
70. *Journal of the House of Representatives of the Eleventh General Assembly* 2:66. See also Lincoln, "Speech on the Sub-Treasury," December 26, 1839, *CW* 1:159–79.
71. *Journal of the House of Representatives of the Eleventh General Assembly* 2:120. See also The Lincoln Log, December 12, 1839; January 2 and 4, 1840.
72. Ibid., January 8, 1840.
73. Lincoln, "Remarks in Illinois Legislature concerning Internal Improvements," January 30, 1840, *CW* 1:201.
74. Miller, *Prairie Politician*, 349.
75. *Illinois State Register*, November 9, 1839.
76. Douglas, *Autobiography*, 340–1.
77. *Sangamo Journal*, January 28, 1840.
78. Lincoln, "A Bill to Repeal 'An Act to Establish and Maintain a General System of Internal Improvements' and All Acts Amendatory Thereto," January 30, 1840, Papers of Abraham Lincoln.
79. Ibid., 177.
80. Pratt, *Personal Finances*, 144.
81. Lincoln, "To John T. Stuart," March 1, 1840, *CW* 1:206.
82. Lincoln, "To John T. Stuart," March 26 1840, *CW* 1:208.
83. Ibid.
84. Lincoln, "To the Editor of the Chicago American," June 24, 1839, *CW* 1:151.
85. Pratt, *Personal Finances*, 100.
86. Burlingame, *Abraham Lincoln*, 95.
87. Herndon and Weik, *Herndon's Lincoln*, 158.
88. Joseph Gillespie to WHH, *Herndon's Informants*, 181.
89. Robert Wilson to WHH, *Herndon's Informants*, 204.
90. Tarbell, *Life of Abraham Lincoln*, 167.
91. *Alton Telegraph*, April 11, 1840.
92. *Illinois State Register*, October 16, 1840.
93. *Belleville Advocate*, April 13, 1840.

94. *Sangamo Journal*, April 6, 1840.

95. Joseph Gillespie to WHH, *Herndon's Informants*, 181.

96. Whitney, *Life on the Circuit*, 127.

97. Ninian Edwards to WHH, *Herndon's Informants*, 447.

98. Burlingame, *Abraham Lincoln*, 150.

99. Lincoln, "To William G. Anderson," October 31, 1840, *CW* 1:211.

100. Herndon and Weik, *Herndon's Lincoln*, 159.

101. Ibid.

102. Lincoln, "To Usher Linder," February 20, 1848, *CW* 1:453.

103. Lincoln, "To Usher Linder," March 22 1848, *CW* 1:458.

104. Gary, *Following in Lincoln's Footsteps*, 13.

105. Michael Burlingame, *The Inner World of Abraham Lincoln* (Urbana: University of Illinois Press, 1994), 237.

106. Wilson, *Honor's Voice*, 210.

6. A Final Term and a Future Undetermined

1. Sandburg, *Prairie Years*, 252.

2. Donald, *Lincoln*, 84–85.

3. Katherine Helm, *The True Story of Mary, Wife of Lincoln* (New York: Harper Publishing Company, 1928), 63–64.

4. Sandburg, *Prairie Years*, 259.

5. Pease, *Illinois Election Returns*, 344.

6. The Lincoln Log, June 2, 1840. See also Howard, *Illinois: History of Prairie State*, 212.

7. Wilson, *Lincoln among His Friends*, 490.

8. Thomas, *Abraham Lincoln*, 78.

9. *Journal of the House of Representatives of the Twelfth General Assembly* 1:5–210.

10. Burlingame, *Abraham Lincoln*, 166.

11. Simon, *Lincoln's Preparation for Greatness*, 228. See Miller, *Prairie Politician*, 413–4.

12. Donald, *A. Lincoln*, 77.

13. *Illinois State Register* (Springfield), December 11, 1840.

14. *Belleville Advocate*, December 12, 1840.

15. *Illinois State Register*, December 11, 1840.

16. Lincoln, "Remarks in the Illinois Legislature concerning Commemoration of the Battle of New Orleans," January 8, 1841, *CW* 1:226.

17. Lincoln, "Speech in Illinois Legislature concerning the State Bank," February 11, 1841, *CW* 1:237–38.

18. Lincoln, "Discussion in Illinois Legislature concerning the State Bank," February 24, 1841, *CW* 1:242–43.

19. Ibid.

20. Ford, *History of Illinois*, 198.
21. Lincoln, "Remarks in Illinois Legislature Amending a Bill Providing Interest on State Debt," December 4, 1840, *CW* 1:215–17.
22. *Journal of the House of Representatives of the Twelfth General Assembly*, 1:10–28.
23. Simon, *Lincoln's Preparation for Greatness*, 235.
24. *Sparta Democrat*, February 12, 1841.
25. *Sangamo Journal*, November 11, 1837.
26. Burlingame, *Abraham Lincoln*, 147.
27. Joshua F. Speed to WHH, *Herndon's Informants*, 430.
28. Burlingame, *Inner World of Abraham Lincoln*, 99.
29. The Lincoln Log, January 18, 1841.
30. Wilson, *Honor's Voice*, 235.
31. Lincoln, "To John T. Stuart," January 23, 1841, *CW* 1:228.
32. The Lincoln Log, January 19, 1841.
33. January 23, 1841, *CW* 1:228.
34. Ibid., 229.
35. Joshua F. Speed to WHH, *Herndon's Informants*, 197.
36. The Lincoln Log, February 3, 1841.
37. Lincoln, "Speech in Illinois Legislature concerning Apportionment," January 9, 1841, *CW* 1:227–28.
38. *Laws of the State of Illinois,* 1840–41 (Springfield: Wm. Walters, 1841), 23.
39. *Journal of the House of Representatives of the Twelfth General Assembly* 1:39–40.
40. Lincoln, "Remarks in Illinois Legislature concerning . . . the Illinois and Michigan Canal," February 26, 1841, *CW* 1:243–44.
41. Ibid.
42. *Journal of the House of Representatives of the Twelfth General Assembly* 1:520–1.
43. *Journal of the House of Representatives of the Twelfth General Assembly* 1:46.
44. "An Act Making Provision for Organizing and Maintaining Common Schools," February 26, 1841, Papers of Abraham Lincoln.
45. Lincoln, "To John T. Stuart," December 17, 1840, *CW* 1:221.
46. *Journal of the House of Representatives of the Twelfth General Assembly* 1:392
47. Ford, *History of Illinois*, 86.
48. *Journal of the House of Representatives of the Twelfth General Assembly*, 1:18–30.
49. *Journal of the House of Representatives of the Twelfth General Assembly*, 1:11.
50. Ibid., 17.

51. Ibid., 136.

52. *Sangamo Journal*, January 3, 1840.

53. Ibid., January 19, 1841.

54. Ford, *History of Illinois*, 262–8. See also Miller, *Prairie Politician*, 429–35.

55. Simon, *Lincoln's Preparation for Greatness*, 248–9. See also Miller, *Prairie Politician*, 18.

56. Lincoln, "Whig Protest . . . against the Reorganization of the Judiciary," February 26, 1841, *CW* 1:245–49.

57. Thomas, *Abraham Lincoln*, 78; Sandburg, *Prairie Years*, 249–50.

58. *Journal of the House of Representatives of the Twelfth General Assembly* 1:161. See also Miller, *Prairie Politician*, 426.

59. *Journal of the House of Representatives of the Ninth General Assembly* 1:161.

60. *Journal of the House of Representatives of the Twelfth General Assembly* 1:562.

61. Simon, *Lincoln's Preparation for Greatness*, 269–71.

62. January 23, 1841, *CW* 1:229–30.

63. Angle, *Here I Have Lived*, 96.

64. *Sangamo Journal*, October 15, 1841.

65. Lincoln, "To Joshua F. Speed," February 25, 1842, *CW* 1:281.

66. *Illinois State Register*, March 25, 1842.

67. "Lincoln to Joshua F. Speed," April 13, 1842, *CW* 1:284–5.

68. Lincoln, "To Frederick A. Thomas," April 21, 1842, *CW* 1:286.

69. Thomas, *Abraham Lincoln*, 78–79; Sutton, "Illinois' Year of Decision," 39.

70. Lincoln, "Speech on the Subtreasury," December 26, 1839, *CW* 1:178.

71. Pratt, *Personal Finances*, 24.

72. Robert H. Browne, *Abraham Lincoln and the Men of His Time* (New York: Eaton and Mains, 1901), 1:245–6.

73. Ralph Waldo Emerson, *Complete Works of Ralph Waldo Emerson* (Cambridge, MA: Riverside Press, 1904), 11:330.

INDEX

Italicized page numbers indicate illustrations.

Clay, Henry, 10–11, 20, 33
Clinton, DeWitt, 31
court-packing efforts by
    Democrats, 122
Cumberland Road, 123

Dawson, John, 21, 53
death penalty, 121
Dement, John, 71
Democratic newspapers, attacks
    on AL, 105–6
Democrats and Democratic Party:
    conventions, national and
    state (1835), 40; court-packing
    efforts, 122–23; plan to end
    special session and kill state
    banks, 114–15; proposition to
    AL, 21; public debates between
    Whigs and, 100; resolution
    aimed at Harrison, 120–21;
    and suffrage for white male
    citizens, 10
de Tocqueville, Alexis, 47–48
Douglas, Stephen A.: on AL, 127;
    AL's debates with, 89, 99–100;
    AL's race against, for U.S.
    Senate, 129; court-packing
    efforts, 122; and Democratic
    state convention, 40; internal
    improvements system and, 57,
    103; Mormons and, 122; run
    for Stuart's seat in Congress,
    88–89; on Sangamon County
    division, 63–65; state supreme
    court appointment, 123; in
    Tenth General Assembly, 51;
    Todd and, 110
Dubois, Jesse K.: as AL's colleague
    in Illinois house, 26; AL's
    friendship with, 125; on AL's
    prominence in first session, 37;
    as AL's roommate during Tenth

Assembly, 50; state capital
    relocation and, 60, 72
Dunbar, Alexander, 71
Duncan, Joseph: abolitionist
    societies and, 74; calls for
    special session of General
    Assembly, 39, 79; internal
    improvements system and,
    27–28, 41, 56, 68–70, 90; on
    new state house in Vandalia, 55;
    on public education, 35–36, 56

Early, Jacob, 49
Edwards, Elizabeth, 110
Edwards, Ninian W.: and AL's
    introduction to Mary Todd,
    110; celebration for passage of
    state capital relocation bill,
    72; Early's duel challenge, 49;
    legislative candidacy of, 44;
    as one of "Long Nine," 53; on
    Sangamon County division
    petitions, 64
Eleventh General Assembly
    (1838–39), 89–98
Elkin, William, 53
Emerson, Ralph Waldo, 127–28
Erie Canal, 31–32
Ewing, William Lee, 43, 94–95

Ficklin, Orlando B., 40–41, 94–95
Fithian, William, 26, 29
Fletcher, Job, 53
Ford, Thomas, 26, 59–60, 72, 126
Forquer, George, 31, 47

Gatewood, W. J., 91
Gillespie, Joseph, 19, 54, 105–6, 114
Graham, Mentor, 3, 6
Green, Bowling, 3, 21, 101
Green, Peter, 95
Gridley, Asahel, 114

Ron J. Keller is an associate professor of history and political science and serves as the managing director of the Abraham Lincoln Center for Character Development at Lincoln College in Lincoln, Illinois. Keller has coauthored several books, including *A Respect for the Office: Letters from the Presidents* and *Abraham Lincoln in Logan County, Illinois, 1834–1860*, and has been a contributor to *White House History* journal. He is a recipient of the Order of Lincoln Award, the highest honor given to a citizen in the state of Illinois.

CONCISE
LINCOLN
LIBRARY

This series of concise books fills a need for short studies of the life, times, and legacy of President Abraham Lincoln. Each book gives readers the opportunity to quickly achieve basic knowledge of a Lincoln-related topic. These books bring fresh perspectives to well-known topics, investigate previously overlooked subjects, and explore in greater depth topics that have not yet received book-length treatment. For a complete list of current and forthcoming titles, see www.conciselincolnlibrary.com.

Other Books in the Concise Lincoln Library

Abraham Lincoln and Horace Greeley
Gregory A. Borchard

Lincoln and the Civil War
Michael Burlingame

Lincoln's Sense of Humor
Richard Carwardine

Lincoln and the Constitution
Brian R. Dirck

Lincoln in Indiana
Brian R. Dirck

Lincoln and the Election of 1860
Michael S. Green

Lincoln and Congress
William C. Harris

Lincoln and the Union Governors
William C. Harris

Lincoln and the Abolitionists
Stanley Harrold

Lincoln's Campaign Biographies
Thomas A. Horrocks

Lincoln and the Military
John F. Marszalek

Lincoln and Emancipation
Edna Greene Medford

Lincoln and Reconstruction
John C. Rodrigue

Lincoln and the Thirteenth Amendment
Christian G. Samito

Lincoln and Medicine
Glenna R. Schroeder-Lein

Lincoln and the Immigrant
Jason H. Silverman

Lincoln and the U.S. Colored Troops
John David Smith

Lincoln's Assassination
Edward Steers Jr.

Lincoln and Race
Richard Striner

Lincoln and Religion
Ferenc Morton Szasz with Margaret Connell Szasz

Lincoln and the Natural Environment
James Tackach

Lincoln and the War's End
John C. Waugh

Lincoln as Hero
Frank J. Williams

Abraham and Mary Lincoln
Kenneth J. Winkle